SCHOOLS IN TRANSITION

SCHOOLS
IN
TRANSITION

Community Experiences in Desegregation

edited by

ROBIN M. WILLIAMS, JR.

AND

MARGARET W. RYAN

CHAPEL HILL

The University of North Carolina Press

MANUFACTURED IN THE UNITED STATES OF AMERICA

Van Rees Press • New York

Preface

THIS BOOK REPORTS SOME OF THE RECENT EXPERIENCES OF twenty-four communities in states bordering the South as they have moved from racially segregated toward integrated public schools.

It aims to be a study based on facts. Within the limits of ordinary human fallibility, it tries to present a balanced account of the situations described. The available evidence is far from complete, and further and more penetrating research is greatly to be desired. Yet where we have so little objective information of any kind it seems quite worthwhile to present the rather specific studies to be summarized here. They are indicative or suggestive rather than conclusive, but they do put on the record a wide range of real experiences with a set of very complicated human problems.

The work is intended for the informed citizen, whether school official or teacher or interested member of a community. It has not attempted to develop a highly technical analysis in sociological or psychological terms. On the other hand, the materials presented perhaps will be of interest to many social scientists.

Part I sketches the general problem of desegregation, with particular attention to the role of law in the patterns of racial separation and integration in American school systems.

Part II treats selected communities in states having "mandatory" laws against segregation. The range of situations existing in these areas helps to illuminate the varying relations between different types of social codes and the actual behaviors supposedly regulated by them. On the other hand, some of the cases reported here show how under particular circumstances legal factors can be of decisive importance.

Part III is mainly concerned with communities that had operated their schools under state laws which permitted either segregation or integration. Again, great variation is apparent in the specific courses of action followed by individual communities.

Part IV briefly summarizes a few main findings and suggests some conclusions that may have applicability beyond the situations studied at first hand for this volume.

The story as it unfolds has its moments of drama and human interest. Its main substance, nevertheless, lies in what it may have to teach us about the working of our society and in what it may imply for a responsible approach to the new problems and opportunities we now face.

This volume owes its first acknowledgment of gratitude to the many school officials, teachers, students, and local citizens, white and Negro, who furnished the vital information about their communities on which are based the twenty-four studies reviewed here.

The editors are deeply appreciative of the work of the scholars who carried out the original field studies. They accomplished a remarkable job of field research under great pressure of time and produced careful, thoughtful reports. Furthermore, their cooperation in critically reviewing the final manuscript was most helpful in correcting errors of fact and interpretation and in improving the perspective of the entire work.

The foresight of the Fund for the Advancement of Education in providing support for these studies warrants strong commendation. In addition, the wise planning and energetic assistance of the Fund's staff, particularly Philip Coombs and John Scanlon, were indispensable to the completion of this work. However, the writing of this book has been the responsibility of the editors. Neither the Fund nor any of its officers or staff members should be held responsible for any errors of fact or for the interpretation of the material presented.

Arrangements for preparation of the volume were greatly facilitated by Mrs. Katherine Riegger, of the Department of Sociology and Anthropology, Cornell University. Finally, we wish to thank the staff of the University of North Carolina Press for their expert aid in seeing the manuscript through final readings and publication.

ROBIN M. WILLIAMS, JR.
MARGARET W. RYAN

Cornell University
Ithaca, New York
July 30, 1954

Contents

PART III

Desegregation Permitted

PART IV

Implications for the Future

Introduction

ON MAY 17, 1954, THE SUPREME COURT OF THE UNITED STATES wrote an end to an era in American education. Before that date the Court had interpreted the Fourteenth Amendment to the Constitution to mean that the several states could educate whites and Negroes separately, provided the facilities made available for the purpose were substantially equal—and seventeen of the forty-eight states, including all those where Negroes were largely concentrated, had required or permitted racial segregation in their public schools. But from May 17 forward, the Court proclaimed, no American could be denied admission to a public educational institution solely because of his race.

There could be no doubt that the Court's unanimous decision removed legal sanction from the practice of segregation in education or that it cleared the way for massive social change. Yet the nature of that change remains clouded with uncertainty. The Court itself recognized that it had left vital questions unanswered when it called for re-argument on the specific decrees to be entered in the five test cases upon which it based the new precedent.

Many of these questions, however, are not legal in character. Many forces have been at work reshaping the character of bi-racial education in the United States—indeed, reshaping the whole of the complex relationship between the majority and minority races. The charting of those forces has been largely left to social scientists, and it is to them the public now must look for guides to the future.

Intensive social studies in the specific field of bi-racial education were already well under way when the Supreme Court handed down its historic decision. They had been undertaken under a grant from the Ford Foundation's Fund for the Advancement of Education, which in the spring of 1953 had recognized the need for a new and comprehensive look at the public school system which had served the two races throughout the nation's history. As a key part of that project, research teams were sent into twenty-four communities which had lately experienced the transition from segregated to integrated schools. These communities, of necessity, were outside the South, for no Southern state had then undertaken to abandon dual education below the college level.

When these field studies reached the project's central research staff in Atlanta, which I served as nominal director, it became apparent that the material thus gathered was far too abundant, and far too valuable, to be compressed into the brief volume originally contemplated. The studies served as the basis for several chapters in the summary report, *The Negro and the Schools*, published (by fortuitous accident, I must confess, and not by design) coincidentally with the Supreme Court decision. But all of us concerned with what came to be called the Ashmore Project felt that they deserved publication in their own right.

Much additional editorial work was necessary, however, to put this raw data together as a coherent picture of American communities in transition. For that essential task we turned to Professor Robin M. Williams, Jr., a native Southerner who is now director of Cornell University's Social Science Research Center and who had served the project as a consultant. In collaboration with Mrs. Margaret W. Ryan, he has prepared this volume for publication.

The purpose of *Schools in Transition* is the same as that of *The Negro and the Schools*—not to argue the case for or against segregation, but to make available factual information which may throw light upon this shadowy area of the nation's total educational structure. Owen J. Roberts, former Associate Justice of the Supreme Court of the United States and now chairman of the Board of The Fund for the Advancement of Education, thus defined the mission of the Ashmore Project in his introduction to the initial volume:

This volume and those that follow it are intended to bring into focus the dimensions and nature of a complex educational problem that in many ways provides a significant test of American democracy. The ultimate solution of that problem will rest with the men and women who make and execute public school policy in thousands of local school districts, and their actions will be conditioned by the degree of understanding of the general public which supports their efforts with its tax dollars. If this project serves to assist them in their task the Fund for the Advancement of Education will feel that it has wisely invested a portion of the risk capital of American education with which it is entrusted.

My thanks, and those of the officers and directors of the Fund, go to Professor Williams and Mrs. Ryan for their skillful preparation of this, the second of the four volumes which represent the end product of the Ashmore Project.

HARRY S. ASHMORE

Little Rock, Arkansas
September 25, 1954

PART I

The Background

CHAPTER 1

What Desegregation Means

THE MATERIAL PRESENTED IN THIS BOOK RELATES TO ONE ASPECT of public school education in the United States: the acceleration of change from a racially segregated to an integrated system. The approach is not that of theory nor of consideration of national politics related to the subject. Rather it represents the actual experiences in twenty-four communities in six states which, since the end of World War II, have moved from some measure of segregation to a system in which Negro and white children attend the same schools. These community studies represent in part a stock-taking, a factual account of what actually occurred during the periods of transition from one system to the other, and an analysis of the specific forces at work in the communities which facilitated or hindered the change in local customary behavior. In a nation with a strong tradition of support for and interest in popular education, the public school system is of major importance to the great majority of parents and to many other citizens and taxpayers. As it touches children, it concerns also the future of the nation.

The public school systems of the United States are tremendous, with some 25 million pupils and over 900,000 teachers, with millions and millions of dollars invested in buildings, grounds, and equipment. These schools are visible evidence of a belief in equality of opportunity for all children. They emphasize a traditionally American conception of the role of education in enabling talent to find its way in the world. Generations of educators and other citizens have believed that a democratic society should provide free public education, up to the university level and in some cases through university, open equally to all children. This has been interpreted as meaning: to the poor and to the well-to-do, to the country boy and his city cousin, to the children of the immigrants of today, and to the descendents of the immigrants who became the first colonial Americans.

That we have not always and everywhere practiced these beliefs is evident to everyone; various gaps between ideals and practices have existed. Contradictions and conflicts have appeared, and these are well illustrated by the problems of segregated schools.

In the thirteen states forming "The South" there has been a dual system from the inception of public education. In this segregated or dual system it has been generally true, until very recently in some localities, that the schools set apart for Negro children have not been the equal of white schools in buildings, grounds, equipment, or the social conditions favorable to optimum learning. What is not so commonly recognized is the situation in the North and West. Many people apparently believe that in these areas there has never been any distinction made between the races for purposes of education and that the same schools have been open to all children living near them. This belief is not justified by the facts.

Residential segregation itself, once established, has resulted in segregated schools in many of the metropolitan areas of the North, where there have been large concentrations of Negro population for many years. In some instances this residential segregation has been forced, reflecting sentiments of the dominant groups in the community; in others it has, in part, "just grown" in the same way that other minority group neighborhoods have developed, with people seeking to live near others of similar backgrounds. The patterns of residential segregation have been facilitated and reinforced by restrictive covenants and other devices. Practices in the real estate business have contributed to this segregation. The ruling of the Supreme Court that restrictive covenants are non-enforceable has not resulted in the disappearance of such agreements. "Civic Improvement Leagues," and the like, have sometimes fostered and maintained restrictive policies.

Some non-Southern communities have used deliberately such devices as gerrymandered school districts, no districts or a "school of choice" policy, separate classrooms, or segregated grades to assure separation of the races. These practices are found most frequently in communities in which the sentiments of dominant groups favor segregation, even sometimes where the law requires an integrated school.

Since the Supreme Court upheld the separate but equal doctrine in the case of *Plessy* v. *Ferguson* in 1896, it has been asked to rule on numbers of individual cases involving the rights of individuals of minority groups in the public schools. Although many of these had to do with the establishment of the right to education without segregation, the rulings, until May 17, 1954, applied to the individual cases involved and were not interpreted in such a way as to apply to all schools and all children in the nation. A series of cases decided by the Supreme Court between 1948 and 1952 opened the doors of graduate and professional schools (such as law) to Negroes living in states which, according to the Court, did not provide equal facilities for Negro students. These decisions affected primarily the state supported universities of the South.

Current interest centers in the effects of the Supreme Court decision in the five cases reviewed in its action of May

17, 1954. These cases involved Negro children in Kansas, South Carolina, Virginia, Delaware, and the District of Columbia. In each of the cases, the legal question concerned some aspect of segregation within the school systems. The points of law under which the cases were decided in the lower courts differed, but the intent of the counsel for the Negroes was clear: to establish as a right *per se* the use of the schools on a non-segregated basis. A reiterated point was that separate could never be equal. However, legal opinion, as well as economic considerations, supported the point that "The fact remains that it will be a far cry from an announcement ... of compelled desegregation ... to the actual issuance of effective judicial orders to the same effect in all the nation's school districts that do not voluntarily comply with the high court's requirements." [1]

The Background

The reversal of the *Plessy* tradition is part of a trend toward the gradual reduction in legally-supported segregation, an indication of an even broader current toward "equality of opportunity," and a move toward making it possible to have integrated participation in the public facilities and the public concerns of the various people of a diverse culture. Many changes have already taken place—dramatic when one considers that as recently as 1940, even those who most ardently wished to see the end of segregation would have said that it was yet impossible in the United States, but pedestrian in the unheralded and prosaic way in which integration came into being.

One important factor in recent American interest in race relations has been the new international role of the country. The twentieth century has seen the rise of the United States

1. Robert A. Leflar and Wylie H. Davis, "Segregation in the Public Schools," *Harvard Law Review*, Vol. 67, No. 3 (January, 1954), p. 420.

to the position of a major world power, with increasing political and economic relations with almost all nations of the world. In international affairs, many of its transactions are with countries whose citizens happen to have darker skins than most Americans do. The people of these countries have been very much aware of segregation and discrimination in the United States. During and since World War II they have repeatedly questioned American motives abroad and pointed to the beam in our eye when the United States has spoken out for equal treatment of all citizens in any nation. The reply that many changes have taken place here in the last hundred years, that gradually these patterns are disappearing, does not always satisfy these critics. They say that the doctrine of Nordic Superiority as espoused by Hitler's Germany (which the United States is said to have gone to war to defeat) and the doctrine of White Supremacy are ideological brothers; they question whether these doctrines are appropriate for a nation which is a leader in advocating democracy abroad.

Not only did the Allies from the other side of the world seriously regard the United States to see how it would operate with peoples of various races or colors, but we began to look around us at home. Many a community became aware, for the first time as a *community*, of the racial tensions which existed at home. Many soldiers, who had accepted ideas of racial superiority, came home from war with the realization that these ideas were not welcomed in most of the modern world.

Another factor in the increased concern with interracial relations was that during the war, the nation found that its potential man power (its population being just 7 per cent of the total world population) was more limited than sheer numbers might indicate. Many individuals could not be used to their full potential capacity—as workers in defense plants, as soldiers or officers, as effective leaders in the local communities—because they did not have the necessary education. With regard to the Armed Forces in World War II, as of May 1, 1944, Selective Service figures showed that 33 per cent of Negro registrants had been rejected as 4-F as against 16 per cent of white registrants. Rejections for most types of physical disabilities or diseases were lower for Negroes than for whites; therefore the greater rejection rate for Negroes seems to be attributed primarily to limitations of education.[2]

As one turns to more recent years, many indices point to the changing status and qualifications of the American Negro, and his increasing participation in the life of the nation as a whole.

In 1950, according to U.S. Census, of the 15 million Negroes in the United States, about 39 per cent lived in states other than the South. Just over three-fifths lived in urban communities. Only one-fifth were classified as rural farm residents. The migration out of the South had assumed significant proportions during and after World War I, with increasingly large settlements in industrial areas of the North and North Central states. Between 1940 and 1950 the Negro population in the South increased 1.5 per cent, while that of the non-South increased 56.6 per cent. World War II created new opportunities in the Northwestern, the North Central, and the Eastern states, where defense plants needed large labor forces. Many communities, which had never before had an appreciable Negro population, acquired a new group to be absorbed into the life of the community.

In each of the states included in this study, both the proportion of Negroes within the state and the actual numbers have increased appreciably since 1940. (See Table 1.) Furthermore, the trend has been for the concentrated Negro settlements in the industrial areas to increase in density,

2. S. A. Stouffer, *et. al., The American Soldier* (Princeton: Princeton University Press, 1949), I, 493-94.

without a proportional increase in the area occupied. One community in this study has noted as much as a 129 per cent increase in the Negro population between 1940 and 1950.

TABLE 1

POPULATION BY RACE, 1950, AND
CHANGE IN NEGRO POPULATION, 1940-1950

Sample States	1950 Population		Change in Negro Population, 1940-1950	
	Total	Negro	Number	Per Cent
Arizona	749,587*	25,974	+10,981	+73.2
Illinois	8,712,176	645,980	+258,534	+66.7
Indiana	3,934,224	174,168	+52,252	+42.9
New Jersey	4,835,329	318,565	+91,592	+40.4
New Mexico	681,187**	8,408	+3,736	+80.0
Ohio	7,946,627	513,072	+173,611	+51.1

* This includes an Indian population of 65,791, or 8.8% of the total.
** Including 41,901 Indians (6.2% of the total).

Source: U. S. Department of Commerce, Bureau of the Census, *Census of the Population: 1950, Vol. II Characteristics of the Population,* Table 14 for each state.

For the South, only four cities (New Orleans, and Amarillo, Galveston, and Wichita Falls, Texas) registered as large a proportional increase in Negro population between 1900 and 1950.[3] While the actual numbers involved in some of the sample cities are not large, it often is the proportional change which is most significant in posing problems in many of the social institutions of the city. (See Table 2.)

A more difficult area to change, but one in which some movement has appeared, is represented by bi-racial housing projects. Studies of those projects which have operated without regard to race, color, or creed indicate that "neighboring" usually takes place between close neighbors whether they are of the same or different background, although con-

3. Harry S. Ashmore, *The Negro and the Schools* (Chapel Hill: The University of North Carolina Press, 1954), pp. 169-71.

TABLE 2

CHANGE IN NEGRO AND TOTAL NON-WHITE POPULATION,
1940-1950, IN THE CITIES STUDIED

State and City	1950 Population			Per Cent Negro, 1950	Per Cent Change, 1940-1950	
	Total	Negro	All Non-White		Negro	All Non-White
Arizona:						
Douglas	9,442	284	251	2.6	9.7	9.1
Nogales	6,153	131	153	2.1	−27.2	−46.7
Phoenix	106,818	5,190	6,621	4.9	21.7	31.3
Tucson	45,454	2,784	3,395	6.1	65.9	37.7
Illinois:						
Cairo	12,123	4,383	4,401	36.1	−20.2	−20.0
Indiana:						
Elkhart	35,646	1,068	1,076	3.0	100.8	100.0
Evansville	128,636	8,483	8,515	6.6	23.6	24.1
Gary	133,911	39,253	39,326	29.3	92.4	92.1
Indianapolis	427,173	63,867	64,091	15.0	24.9	25.1
Jeffersonville	14,685	1,904	1,905	13.1	59.5	59.5
New Albany	29,346	1,301	1,304	4.4	6.1	6.4
South Bend	115,911	8,134	8,227	7.0	128.8	128.1
New Jersey:						
Atlantic City	61,657	16,782	16,862	27.2	7.1	7.1
Burlington	12,051	1,956	1,958	16.2	43.6	43.7
Camden	124,555	17,434	17,583	14.1	39.7	40.2
Mount Holly	8,206	463	471	5.6	N.A.	N.A.
Salem	9,050	1,847	1,851	20.4	19.9	20.2
New Mexico:						
Alamogordo	6,783	211	220	3.1	74.4	78.9
Carlsbad	17,975	554	573	3.1	74.8	80.8
Clovis	17,318	616	637	3.6	116.9	95.4
Hobbs	13,875	1,350	1,353	9.7	122.4	113.4
Las Cruces	12,325	288	300	2.3	14.3	14.1
Roswell	24,738	792	817	3.1	67.1	72.4
Ohio:						
Cincinnati	503,998	78,196	78,685	15.5	40.7	40.2

Source: United States Census, 1940 and 1950.
N.A.—not available.

tacts with residents in other buildings or sections of the project tend to remain impersonal.[4]

In the Northern metropolitan centers, where the Negro residential areas are usually in the older sections of the city, the schools often are older buildings without many of the facilities now considered necessary for the school program. In some cases these schools have operated on a segregated basis until fairly recently; in many others the ratio of Negroes to whites has been large. Nevertheless, these schools have enabled the Negro children who attended them to get a "better education," by accepted general standards, than would have been available in the rural areas of the South. In the smaller communities of the North and West, where the actual number of Negroes did not warrant the establishment of separate facilities, integrated schools were usual until the 1920's and 1930's saw a revival of racial animus exemplified by such movements as the Ku Klux Klan. For a time the tendency was then toward some system of segregation, either by elementary schools or by segregated classes within them. Rarely in such instances were the high schools segregated. This pattern began to change rapidly after the end of World War II when more and more communities integrated the entire school system.

For the most part, the recent changes have meant that Negro children have had a greater opportunity to acquire an education fitting them for skilled or professional work. Some who took advantage of this were then faced with restrictions regarding employment availability, but the general educational level of Negroes has risen markedly, and there has developed a much larger Negro middle and upper class of skilled and professional workers.

The first breaches in segregated higher education in the

4. Cf. for example, Morton Deutsch and M. E. Collins, *Interracial Housing, A Psychological Study of a Social Experiment* (Minneapolis: University of Minnesota Press, 1951).

South were watched by some with fear, and predictions of riots were common. The actual change came about quietly, with little public attention. This change, involving as it did primarily graduate and professional schools, has not yet added many Negro students to schools formerly for whites only, but those who have taken advantage of the new educational opportunities have, for the most part, been accepted in the classroom and on the campus.

With only a few exceptions, the pattern [is] official resistance to Negro admission until, voluntarily or as the result of court action, the admission policy is changed; even-handed application of administrative policies once Negroes are admitted.[5]

And now the public schools are becoming part of the movement toward a redefinition of "equal rights."

Opportunities for employment have also broadened since the beginning of the last war. Several states have enacted fair employment practices laws or have revitalized civil rights laws in the effort to open employment opportunities for individuals without regard to color, race, religion, or national origin. Discrimination still exists on a large scale, but many industries and firms have found that a non-discriminatory policy works well within the organization and also is profitable in business terms. Negroes are being upgraded more frequently and in greater numbers as they demonstrate ability in the jobs to which they are assigned, and the indication is that this trend is more likely to continue than to reverse direction. To date, these changes involve a small proportion of employable Negroes, but this proportion is increasing. Business men are paying more attention to the growing market for quality products among Negroes. This not only reflects a higher economic status, but also preferences and consumption patterns affected by the higher level of education.

5. Harry Ashmore, *op. cit.*, p. 42.

In another sphere of national life, the votes of Negro citizens have become important. That these votes could influence the outcome of elections has been recognized in the metropolitan centers of the North for many years, but it is only within the last decade that outlawing of the white primary, repeal of poll tax laws, and other changes have made the Negro vote important in some of the Southern states. These changes have helped to open the way to political participation by Negroes. Roughly 1½ million of about 6 million adult Negroes voted in the 1952 elections. Such participation is increasingly evident not only in national elections, but also at the state and local levels. As a result, the interests of Negroes and of some other minority groups now more often are represented in state legislatures, offices of education, on local boards of education, city councils, county and municipal police forces, and other elected bodies or other units of government.

Perhaps the most complete change from segregation to integration has occurred in the Armed Forces of the United States since World War II. Patchy and piecemeal as the process was in the beginning, it has now gone far toward completion. Desegregation in this instance has been supported by individuals and groups of widely different attitudes and affiliations. The main initial resistance within the Armed Forces seems to have given way before such evidence as the record of performance of integrated units in Korea, as well as the indications of more efficient use of manpower for the Armed Forces. What was approached as a daring experiment is now widely regarded as militarily more effective than the former system of segregation.

These social changes have not been revolutionary or dramatic. They have occurred slowly and, for many individuals and groups, painfully. A new factor is the *acceleration of the rate of change*. Some of the changes are more apparent than real, it is true, in that they affect only a small proportion of the total American Negro population. However, this does not minimize the importance of recent changes, for the legal disabilities which are being removed and the local practices of discrimination which are giving way to equal treatment are significant changes in the institutional aspects of American life, that is, in the accepted social arrangements for meeting basic requirements of the general population, i.e., school, church, and public facilities.

In the aspects of community life not regulated by laws, there is perhaps less apparent change from the traditional customs. It has often happened that people of different racial or cultural backgrounds have met and have worked together without a marked inclination to carry their association over into all informal social situations. Thus, although all children may go to the same schools and get along well together in work and at play on the school grounds, this may not carry over into the after-school activities of the different groups.

The Communities Studied

This book is about processes sometimes called *desegregation* and sometimes *integration*. Both words presuppose the fact that schools are not everywhere and at all times available on the same terms to all children. *Segregation* is the general term for a *system* of separation, whether legally required or informally maintained, of children or school officials of different "racial," religious, or nationality backgrounds. This study refers mainly to the separation of children who are considered to be "Negroes" and children who are considered to be "whites," although it will be noted that in the Southwestern part of the United States children of Spanish-American and Indian descent also sometimes have been segregated. By *desegregation* is meant any process of bringing Negro (or other "non-white") and white children into the same schools: this sharing of schools involves bi-racial classes, and in some cases bi-racial faculties and administration. It also refers to bi-racial PTA's and other school organiations. *Integration,* on the other hand, has to do with the participation of Negroes and whites in the same activities, with a maximum of cooperation. When integration has been fully accomplished, this common participation is taken for granted as normal and customary. Integration includes bi-racial extra-curricular and school-related activities, as well as classroom activities.

The present question is not whether integration will come, but how it will come and when. Laws can smooth the way, relieve suppressed feelings of guilt on the one hand and inferiority on the other, and they give support to those who are willing to change. Laws may also increase tensions and conflicts. In the communities considered here, many public officials who did not themselves share the attitudes of the more "conservative" members of their communities have hesitated to move without firm legal backing. Once assured of strong legal support, they were able to work toward complete integration more quickly than they earlier had thought possible. Threats of community reprisals, i.e., withdrawals from public schools, riots, boycotts, etc., were seldom carried out, as the material to be presented will show. At the time of these studies, made during the late summer of 1953, very few children had been withdrawn from the public schools that were examined, as a result of a change in school policy. On the whole, the communities studied were law-abiding, even if sometimes restive.

Since the South has the most at stake—financially in the need for improved and expanded facilities, and emotionally, in the prospect of changing to a system different from the traditional pattern—the states included in the study are those with a "Southern exposure." The financial burden of a dual school system, as well as the current pressures on moral and legal grounds, led some communities to consider integration of schools before the recent Supreme Court decision. The possibility of a ruling which would force the issue also had entered earlier into the thinking of school officials, even in cities which would otherwise have been opposed to any consideration of change. These cities are ones whose citizens come from both North and South, whose customs reflect both sections of the country. They, too, are states which have had a large in-migration of Southern Negroes in the last decade. In some of the communities studied, Negroes have become an integral part of the local population only recently. It will be apparent as the material is presented that even within the same state there are conflicting practices and customs, that some communities have not resisted the process, while others have tried various methods to circumvent integration.

It is well recognized that changes in one institutional aspect of a community may focus temporarily many diverse and conflicting interests on the operation of that particular part of community life. Once an "issue" has been posed, the final outcome may bear little resemblence to the problem as it was first raised. Diverse motives and interests become involved in very complicated ways. Yet in the cases of desegregation studied here such clusterings of various personal relationships, vested interests, and the accompanying hopes and fears seem to have had little staying power. Opponents of desegregation did not form permanently organized blocs. The participants in early resistance often appeared to have little else in common to hold them together. School officials considering the method of desegregation to be followed found that they were subject to pressures from diverse groups, that such pressures polarized the community pro and con temporarily, but that once a definite policy was established, the normal functioning of the schools was of no further unusual or dramatic interest to the community residents.

Collectively the communities studied represent experience in many aspects of the process. These studies cover the spectrum of likely types of responses. They show, for instance, what kinds of publicity appear to have been helpful, what kinds more nearly a hindrance to the school administration. They furnish examples of the role of the school board, the superintendent, and other school officials before, during, and after the policy was announced, with particular emphasis on the key role played by the superintendent. They suggest the nature of decision-making power in communities. They indicate the different problems encountered in gradual or step-by-step desegregation, as contrasted with immediate and decisive change.

These studies also supply some facts which may place the process in its broader perspective. The fact that school desegregation is only one facet of the more comprehensive reduction in discriminatory practices now under way may mean that ultimately it will be accepted as matter-of-fact, usual and customary. That it directly involves only the formal and regulated segments of school life may reassure some officials. It is amply demonstrated in these communities that predictions of what will happen as the result of these changes are usually much more pessimistic than later events would have justified.

Some qualifications should be kept in mind. Segregation, whether in the schools or in other institutional aspects of community life, is not and never has been a Southern monopoly. The communities here studied are not in the South, but they have enough similarities in customary behavior patterns to be suggestive. The segregated residential areas reflect similar attitudes in many cases. Employment practices are only somewhat more liberal than in the South. Use of public parks and swimming pools is often on a segregated basis. While some states by law require equal access to places of amusement, theaters, and restaurants, Negroes are frequently hesitant to avail themselves of the right through anticipation of discourteous service.

The case studies do not claim to be exhaustive, but it is hoped that they high-light the major factors involved in each community and reflect accurately the behavior of the residents during the process of desegregation.

The information to be presented refers to twenty-four communities in six states, constituting a great arc on the northern rim of the Southern states. During August and September, 1953, field workers gathered information first-hand in each of them, using as their sources of information the school officials, city and county officials, interracial agencies, and informed adults and school pupils of both races. The communities in New Mexico were visited in the summer of 1954, in a follow-up on the earlier study. Wherever possible, students of both races were interviewed to ascertain their reactions to the program from the point of view of participation or resistance.

The communities were as large as Cincinnati, and as small as Nogales, Arizona, or the villages surveyed in southern New Jersey. They represent both industrial and non-industrial areas, from Camden, New Jersey, to Cairo, Illinois. They reflect the customs of such differing regions of the United States as the Southwest—Arizona and New Mexico; the Midwest—Illinois, Indiana, and Ohio; and the East—New Jersey. The size of the Negro population varied from large to small, and from a large per cent of the total to a very small per cent. In some cases the proportion of Negro to white has been relatively stable, in others it has increased noticeably in the last decade. The pattern of housing varied from highly segregated, ghetto-like districts to a rather random and scattered arrangement.

In analyzing the results of the field information, additional data were drawn on as they proved useful. The additional sources included the laws under which the states operated;

statistical records for the communities, such as population composition, economic levels, school statistics, and the like; and other studies of a comparable nature, such as the Cornell University research in intergroup relations [6] and Tipton's study of the school strikes in Gary, Indiana.[7]

The case studies have been divided into two sections. The first (Part II) deals with communities in states which had laws requiring integrated schools. In this part the material is arranged to show what happened in communities which tried immediate desegregation at all levels of the public schools and what occurred in those which attempted to move gradually toward the goal of total integration. Part III deals mainly with communities in states whose law was permissive rather than mandatory. First the communities which integrated completely, in spite of legal permission for segregation, are discussed; then those which moved more hesitantly or partially toward desegregation are reported. There are some exceptions to the rule within this part of the book. One small southern New Jersey community is included in the latter part of the book because, although it was "required" to integrate the schools, it moved only reluctantly and slowly in this direction.

The legal criterion was used as the basis of presentation of the case studies because it seemed the most objective way of ordering the data. There is no implication that one type of law is necessarily more effective than another or that integration can be assured only under some particular kind of compulsory law. All that is implied is that the law in fact sets the limits under which the individual communities frame their own practices and policies. Thus, the laws which required segregation have effectively prevented school adminis-

6. A series of studies, supported by the Rockefeller Foundation; results are now being prepared for publication.

7. James H. Tipton, *Community in Crisis, The Elimination of Segregation from a Public School System* (New York: Bureau of Publications, Teachers College, Columbia University, 1953).

trators from making changes and at the same time have illustrated the dilemma of those who thought that time would take care of the problem without any active program on the part of interested citizens.

In this context the field studies summarize a variety of approaches to the realistic problems of effective desegregation. The research shows in certain detailed and concrete ways how complex the solutions may be. It also demonstrates that relatively simple and clear policies often make the processes of integration practicable in ordinary American communities. Only at the end of the examination of the record will there emerge a total picture of the implications or the possible applications to the communities now legally required to modify their former procedures.

CHAPTER 2

State Laws Set Limits

THE RECENT SUPREME COURT DECISION AGAINST SEGREGATION in the public schools places this chapter in its proper historical perspective: a review of the way in which some states handled this particular aspect of public school education in the decade before the reversal of the "separate but equal" doctrine laid down by the *Plessy* case more than a half century earlier.

The community studies are grouped in two main classes, on the basis of whether the state law was mandatory or permissive concerning the policy to be followed by the local school authorities as to segregation or integration of the schools. There is, as has been said, no implication that the law as such could determine in detail the local administration of the schools. However, state constitutions, statutes, common law or court decisions set certain boundaries within which each community created the pattern of the schools. That individual communities, operating under the same state law could, and did, interpret it in many different ways will be abundantly demonstrated throughout the book. That the Southern states, now asked to amend their prevailing practices, will find many individual ways to interpret the ruling, both on the state and the local level, seems a safe prediction.

Of the states which border the South, three (Arizona, New Mexico, Kansas) in 1953 permitted but did not require segregation. Nebraska, which just touches a corner of Missouri, has no legislation concerning this aspect of public school administration, but the prevailing pattern has been one of integration. In the remaining seven states (Colorado, Iowa, Illinois, Indiana, Ohio, Pennsylvania, New Jersey) segregation was prohibited, either entirely or partially. In three of these (Colorado, Iowa, Pennsylvania) integrated schools have been common, although certainly not universal, for many years; no communities from these states were included in the sample.

The four states for which community studies will be presented in Part II—Indiana, Illinois, New Jersey, Ohio—required integrated schools. The requirements varied in specificity and in the legal power for enforcement. Each state has had a long history of ambivalence toward racial segregation, and each within recent years has enacted legislation apparently intended to assure a non-segregated school system. Historically, these states have combined a cultural "Southern exposure" with emphasis on universal opportunity for public education, at least in terms of official policy. The result has been that over the years the laws governing the schools have varied from a policy of complete segregation to one of complete integration, with practically every possible combination in use in some community at any one time. Where local sentiment was thought to be opposed to desegregated schools, various administrative devices were employed to avoid compliance with the law. In the group of states with mandatory laws here considered, with the exception of Indiana, the most recent legislation prohibiting segregation has incorporated definite provisions for enforcement.

The enforcement clauses employed three different techniques or combinations of these. In Illinois and New Jersey, state financial aid could be withheld from counties not obeying the law. New Jersey had the additional provision that an individual who was discriminated against might appeal directly to the proper state agency. In Indiana there was no provision in the law to assure its enforcement, and one result was conflicting local interpretation of the intent of the law. Ohio provided fines between $50 and $500 or imprisonment of not less than thirty days or more than ninety days, or both, for violation of its statute. While individual community responses to the desegregation process varied widely, it seemed that those states with a strong enforcement clause, implemented at the state level, came closer to an integrated school system than did states with no enforcement clause or a permissive law. The end product—desegregation or integration—appeared to be related both to the state legal position and to the particular practices and sentiments of individual communities in regard to minority groups.

States Which Prohibited Segregation

Ohio. The history of legal regulation in Ohio is illustrative of the changing and varied solutions attempted on the perimeter of the South. The Ohio laws of 1828-1829 expressly denied Negroes the benefit of free schools. In 1847 this was changed to *permit* the maintenance of separate schools for Negroes. A year later the legislature made it possible to use taxes paid by white residents for the maintenance of schools for Negroes. In 1853 the law was revised to require the allocation of public school funds in proportion to the number of children of school age regardless of color.[1]

But the story continued to be complex. Six years later a case carried to the Ohio Supreme Court resulted in a ruling that the school law did not entitle Negro children, *as a right,*

1. *Brief for Appellants in Nos. 1, 2 and 4 and for the Respondents in No. 10 on Reargument,* Supreme Court of the United States, October term, pp. 170-71.

to admission at schools for whites. It was not until 1878 that a law was passed which *permitted* rather than *required* segregated schools. The final act of this nineteenth-century legal saga came in 1887 when the former legislation was revised to require integrated schools.[2] However, as the study of Cincinnati will show, some segregated schools continued to be used and some new ones were built from time to time.

Following World War II, new forces left their trace in the 1948 revision of the Ohio Code Annotated. The former Civil Rights law had included schools among other places which could not practice discrimination. Mention of schools was deleted from the 1948 revision, although the Civil Rights law is still referred to in some cases of discrimination in schools. (See Appendix I.) Apparently it was felt that specific laws relating to the schools sufficiently protected the rights of minorities.

Thus, from the 1820's to the 1940's those standards of human conduct called laws had gone from express denial of the right of Negroes to public education all the way to the position that any denial of access was a punishable offense against the social order. Whatever the local practices, this history is an important example of change in the dominant institutions and symbols which set the background for each community's resolution of the "American dilemma."

Indiana. Turning now to a second state, there is a similarly fascinating history of changing social values. In Indiana the law of 1853 specified that no Negro nor mulatto should "derive any of the benefits of the common schools of the state." The education committee explained its action, saying that it was "held better for the weaker party that no privilege be extended to them, the tendency of which might be to induce the belief that the prejudices of the dominant race could ever be mollified so much as to break down the rugged barriers that must forever exist between their social rela-

2. *Ibid.*, pp. 171-72.

tions." [3] By 1869 the impact of the War between the States was reflected in an act to "render taxation for common-school purposes uniform, and to provide for the colored children of the state." Eight years later a new addition to the law specified that if there were no schools provided for Negroes, they should be allowed to attend the public schools with white children.

In 1877 there were over 10,000 Negro children in the state, and over two-thirds of them went to the public schools. By 1890 there were more than 150 schools for Negroes in Indiana, with approximately 20,000 pupils. From 1877 to 1949 the local school boards could decide whether the elementary or secondary schools, both or neither, were to be segregated. Again, all the possible combinations were tried in different parts of the state. For example, at the same time that a separate high school for Negroes was being built in one city, a similar school was closed in another city and the Negro students sent to another school attended by white children only.

The trend toward separate schools for whites and Negroes was accelerated in the 1920's when among the communities studied, the schools, notably in Indianapolis, came under the influence of the Ku Klux Klan. The alleged "Klan control" of Indiana schools was broken in the 1930's, and during World War II a movement to change the state law gained momentum. Meanwhile a series of school "strikes" or mass truancy in Gary focused attention on the six-year plan for integration of the schools there. A similar strike in Indianapolis in September, 1948, was condemned by the *Indianapolis Star* which said, "Most reasonable white persons in the city know that the mixing of races in our schools is the just and economical way to run the school system."

In 1949 a bill was presented in the legislature providing

3. Richard G. Boone, *A History of Education in Indiana* (New York: D. Appleton and Co., 1892), pp. 237-38.

for integrated schools throughout the state. A similar bill had been defeated in 1947, but this one was passed and signed by the governor. Although the law is very detailed and apparently specific in its provisions, there has been much discussion of the full meaning of these provisions and the best way of implementing them. No provision for enforcement was incorporated into the bill, which possibly may go far to account for the alleged violations of it. For those who wish to examine a classic example of detailed legislation without strong enforcement provisions, the law is quoted in full in Appendix II. Essentially it provides in sweeping and specific terms that there shall be no discrimination or separation on the basis of race, color, or creed in public schools, colleges, and universities in the state of Indiana, nor in the transportation of public school pupils and students.

That this extraordinarily detailed legislation has been subject to many varied interpretations is, indeed, food for thought. Specific and detailed as the law is, it did not establish at the same time an agency for enforcing it, nor did it indicate what means were to be used to make it effective. Thus, it was possible for Indianapolis to consider that junior high schools were actually elementary schools and thus to delay the integration process at that level. In Evansville it was possible to keep schools for Negroes as "open" schools and allow school of choice to all children, with the burden of choice on the parents in each case. Some critics thought that the confusion surrounding the bill stemmed from its application of gradualism—desegregation by stages rather than a complete change at one time.

Illinois. In the third state requiring integrated schools, Illinois, there was not in early times a specific law on segregation, but legislation passed in 1858 provided that school districts with Negro populations should provide the Negroes a portion of the school fund equal to the amount of taxes collected from them. This was interpreted as justifying the maintenance of segregated schools.[4] In 1874 the first law specifically relating to the exclusion of Negro children was passed, providing fines for maintaining segregated schools. (See Appendix III.)

These statutes governed the schools until 1909, when two more provisions were added, covering the powers of school boards in assigning pupils to schools. In 1945 these two provisions were amended to assure desegregation of public schools. (See Appendix IV.)

It was reported to political authorities that in spite of these additions to the law, some southern counties in Illinois continued to segregate pupils according to race. Therefore, in 1949, the legislature passed the Jenkins amendment to the school appropriations bill, which provided that "No part of the money appropriated by this act shall be distributed to any school district in which any student is excluded from or segregated in any public school, within the meaning of 'The School code,' because of race, color or nationality." [5]

The state superintendent of schools asked the attorney general to rule that "responsibility for certification as to whether schools were segregated should rest upon the local County Superintendent of Schools." He so ruled. In this respect the enforcement clause has been interpreted quite differently than that of New Jersey, where enforcement is the responsibility of a state agency. The local county superintendents in Illinois, being both elected officials and resident in the communities they serve, are thus invested with heavy responsibility.

New Jersey. The last state in this sample which recently prohibited segregation, New Jersey, also had an early law (1844) establishing a public school system "for the equal benefit of all persons," but another law in 1850 gave Morris Township the right to establish a separate school for Negroes,

4. Supreme Court Brief, *op. cit.*, pp. 173-74.
5. Ill. Stats., 1949, p. 53, H. B. 1066.

and this was interpreted as allowing segregated schools any-where in the state. By 1870 the school law was amended to provide for a "thorough and effective system of public schools for the instruction of all children." Nevertheless, segregated schools continued to be the rule rather than the exception in the southern counties of the state.[6]

Social changes as complex as those under consideration in this book seldom can be traced to a single cause. However, a single precipitating factor sometimes brings other contribut-ing causes into focus and may thus galvanize hitherto weak, ineffective forces into a combination that makes organized affirmative action possible. A clear unequivocal statement of public policy, backed by the determination and resources necessary to enforce it, may serve to focus and release com-plex social forces in just this way. This appears to have been the case in New Jersey.

During 1947 a constitutional convention was called to revise the constitution of the state. The revised constitution was submitted to a state-wide referendum and adopted in November of 1947 with the provision that it should become effective in January of 1948. Included in this document was the following clause which established the authority for, and the goals to be sought in, the subsequent process of public school desegregation:

No person shall be denied the enjoyment of any civil or military right, nor be discriminated against in the exercise of any civil or military right, nor be segregated in the militia or in the public schools, because of religious scruples, race, color, ancestry or national origin.[7]

This provision is unique as a statement of public policy of a sovereign state of the United States in that it forbids by its charter segregation *per se* because of minority status in

6. Supreme Court Brief, *op. cit.*, pp. 167-68.
7. Constitution of New Jersey, Revised, 1947, Art. 1, sec. 5.

its public schools. While several other states have legislated against *discrimination* in the provision of educational opportunities by public school institutions, none other than New Jersey has declared that segregation in itself is a violation of the state law. In this way New Jersey became the only state whose law coincides exactly in apparent intent with the recent Supreme Court decision. In New Jersey, segregation became *prima facie* evidence of discrimination, and the widely held criterion of "separate but equal" facilities was rendered irrelevant.

The enforcement agency for this part of the constitution was already present in the Department of Education's Division against Discrimination (DAD). This division had been established in 1945 under the law against discrimination and given the responsibility to "prevent and eliminate discrimination in employment against persons because of race, creed, color, national origin or ancestry by employers, labor organizations, employment agencies or other persons and to take other actions against discrimination because of race, creed, color, national origin or ancestry. . . ." [8]

Two other laws support the provision of the constitution and the Law against Discrimination as amended in 1949 by the Freeman Act. These provided punishment for the exclusion of any child from any school on account of religion, nationality, or color; they also provided that teachers could not be dismissed solely on these grounds.[9] (See Appendix V.)

Within these four states which required a non-segregated school system, fourteen communities have been studied for this book to see what happened as the desegregation process was started, what the community reactions were throughout the process, and what kinds of problems the school administration was called on to solve. The city selected in Ohio was

8. New Jersey Law, 1945, c. 169, p. 589, sec. 6.
9. L. 1903 (2d Sp. Sess.), c. 1, sec. 125, p. 48 (C. S. p. 4767, sec. 125) as amended L. 1945, c. 172, p. 601, sec. 1.

Cincinnati, which had a longer history of integration than any other included in the sample. The communities in Indiana were Elkhart, Evansville, Gary, Indianapolis, Jeffersonville, New Albany, and South Bend. Cairo was selected in Illinois, in part because of the prominence given to the initial disturbances there when the schools were desegregated. New Jersey communities included Atlantic City, Burlington, Camden, Mount Holly, and Salem. Each of these, except Mount Holly, will be discussed in some detail in Part II.

States Which Permitted Integration

The two Southwestern states in the sample—New Mexico and Arizona—are also states which have large Spanish-American or Mexican-American and Indian populations but relatively small Negro populations. In each of these states, at different times, both the Indian and the Spanish-American children have been required to attend segregated schools. The patterns of settlement and the individual histories of the states have influenced legislation in the past.

The New Mexico constitution provides that there shall be "a uniform system of free public schools sufficient for the education of, and open to, all children of school age in the state...." [10] However, nothing is said there about separate schools for minority groups. In 1923, during a period of "anti-alien" reaction, a law was passed which permitted segregated schools if the local school board, with permission from the state board, felt that the best interests of pupils would be so served. However, the law required that facilities be equal. (See Appendix VI.)

Both New Mexico and Arizona segregated first grades for pupils coming from homes in which Spanish is spoken, but these classes are not considered segregated in the same sense as those in which Negro pupils were set apart. It is considered

10. New Mexico Constitution, 1911, Art. 12, sec. 1.

by school officials in the state to be good pedagogy to instruct these children as a group, with emphasis on the use of English as well as on the content of instruction the first year, so that they may progress faster in the regular classes the following years.

Until 1951 the Arizona law permitted the segregation of Negro children in the elementary schools, and in high schools where there were more than twenty-five Negro students.

The first segregation law in Arizona was adopted in 1909 by the Territorial Legislature. This law (Section 54-516 of the Arizona Code) outlined the powers and duties of school trustees: "The Board shall segregate pupils of the African race from pupils of the Caucasian race in all schools other than high schools, and provide all accommodations made necessary by such segregation." Section 54-430 enlarged the board of trustees' powers of segregation by stating, ". . . they may segregate groups of pupils and may maintain special schools during vacation as necessary for the pupils of the district."

Segregation of high school pupils could be accomplished by the school trustees under the provisions of either of two sections in the law (Section 54-430 or 54-918), provided there were twenty-five or more Negroes registered for high school.

In November, 1950, an initiative measure to abolish segregation was put before the voters of the state. It was one of thirteen measures being voted on at the same time, and the other issues had powerful opposition. The measures were defeated by a two to one majority although supporters of the school bill claimed that their measure was not so completely rejected.

In 1951 a bill similar to the defeated measure was introduced into the legislature. It was amended to make segregation permissive rather than mandatory, passed, and signed by the governor. The wording of the clause pertaining to segregation read, "The board of trustees may segregate groups of pupils in all schools other than high schools, and provide all accommodations made necessary by such segregation." This wording removed mention of race as a basis of segregation. At the same time, segregated high schools were prohibited by the repeal of Section 54-918, mentioned above.

Under the laws of these two states, then, one could expect to find and did find both segregated and integrated elementary schools. Only a conviction that integration was the "right approach" to education for all children would, under these laws, make a town change its customary manner of operation.

In New Mexico the six communities studied were Clovis, Las Cruces, Roswell, Alamogordo, Carlsbad, and Hobbs. In Arizona there were four: Douglas, Nogales, Phoenix, and Tucson. These communities are discussed in Part III.

This, then, was the legal situation in these states as the Supreme Court handed down its momentous decision. Can their experiences in framing laws to implement desegregation, and the processes of desegregation as they developed in the individual communities, serve in any way to suggest courses of decision and action for the rest of the nation in the period of transition now upon us?

PART II

Desegregation Required

CHAPTER 3

The Gradual Approach:

CINCINNATI, OHIO *

CINCINNATI HAS A LONGER CONTINUOUS HISTORY OF INTERRACIAL schools than any other community included in this study. Not only the Ohio Equal Rights Law of 1887 [1] but also the city's own policy prohibit compulsory segregation of public school students. However, this present and prevailing policy of maintaining one integrated school system has not always been enforced. The fact of prior segregation makes the recent successful experience with an integrated system in this large industrial city worthy of note by other communities in which —even as in Cincinnati—the people also may have ambivalent feelings toward public school desegregation. At times in the past the Cincinnati school authorities were subjected to allegations of gerrymandering districts to keep white children out of schools predominantly for Negroes, of allowing transfers out of the home district, of assigning "troublesome" Negro pupils to all-Negro schools, and of using other devices to avoid, without actually disobeying, the state law. Within the last decade these charges have been heard less frequently, and there is much testimony in the city to the effect that

* Based on the report of field research prepared by Milton Yinger, Oberlin College. (This original report, as well as those on which following chapters are based, is on file with the Fund for the Advancement of Education).

1. See Chapter 2, pp. 23-24.

the actual administration of the schools is in keeping with the spirit as well as the letter of the law. That this changed practice may have worked also to lessen friction in other areas of race relations in the city will appear as the report develops.

Cincinnati has been described as "a Northern city with a Southern exposure." Its industrial pattern, its political affiliations, and many of its traditions make it part of the Northern region. The middle and particularly the upper socioeconomic classes have been "Northern" in origin and inclinations. The people with lower incomes have a closer identification with the South, many of them being fairly recent migrants from Kentucky, West Virginia, Tennessee, and Alabama. Another Southern characteristic is the presence of a large farm population in the surrounding region which would normally support conservative attitudes. Unlike many other industrial cities it has relatively few foreign-born persons (4 per cent). This juxtaposition of North and South has helped to produce the balance of forces which characterize the pattern of race relations in the city.

For many years the practice in Cincinnati has been to maintain a formally integrated school system. However, there have been some important exceptions to this practice, in the form of four schools for Negroes. The first such school was in a predominantly white upper middle-class neighborhood, Walnut Hills. It was started at the turn of the century. As the Basin, a crowded down-town area, became the center of the Negro population, three more schools appeared there shortly after World War I.

Beginning about 1940 evidence of a new concern with integration appeared and was signaled by the establishment of the Mayor's Friendly Relations Committee in 1943, interracial workshops, and other civic organizations working in this field. The third period of development was characterized by a series of specific moves toward integration, beginning in 1944 and extending to the present time. During the most recent period, changes in the educational system have been accompanied by scattered but significant reductions in segregation in other areas of community life. It will be apparent from the more detailed discussion which follows that this long and complicated set of historical developments is extremely important as an aid to an understanding of the present situation.

The integration of public schools is not complete even today. The school for Negroes started in Walnut Hills about fifty years ago was meant, in part at least, to take care of the children of servants in the middle- and upper-class white families there. Although no child was required to attend, children from several school districts went there and all were, and are, Negro children. In recent years Negroes began to move into Walnut Hills. They now constitute about half the residents of the area.

After World War I three more schools for Negroes were established in the Basin. The Basin is the area of concentration of Negro people in the heart of the city, and these schools were the result of the efforts of a Negro teacher who felt that the adjustments of rural migrant youth could best be served by a school geared to their particular needs and abilities.

Until recently facilities in the schools attended predominantly or exclusively by Negro children were somewhat older and less attractive than those in the white districts, but this seems to have been more nearly a function of residential segregation and the direction of urban growth than of deliberate policy. It was uneconomic to replace these older buildings when expansion in suburban areas necessitated the construction of new facilities. Recently, however, a new elementary and a new junior high school have been opened in the Basin. The faculties in these schools are almost evenly divided between Negro and white teachers while about 95 to 99 per cent of the students are Negro. Occasionally the charge is made that new schools are being built in areas where the population is rapidly becoming entirely Negro, thus "planning for future segregation." This charge is contradicted by the strong stand the local school administration takes against segregation. It might justifiably be said that the school board has not used the changing population situation to redistrict the schools in such a way as to insure a maximum of bi-racial schools ("inverted gerrymandering"), but there has been effective official action against segregation.

The administration still maintains two eligibility lists for teachers, although salaries are on a city-wide scale. In spite of a teacher shortage there are at least a few well-qualified Negro teachers who are not employed. Some of the schools having many Negro students do not yet have integrated faculties. Until 1944 the only Negro teachers and principals were in the schools attended only by Negroes. The training of the teachers and the size of the classes are approximately equal, so far as can be judged.

It seems unnecessary to labor the point that the climate created during World War II focused attention, national and local, on American minority groups and their participation in several aspects of the American way of life. In places such as Cincinnati which already had a potentially effective legal mechanism for enforcing non-segregation, it was relatively easy for civic organizations to increase their influence on the civil as well as the privately owned community facilities to see that the law was upheld with a minimum of friction. In 1952 the first conviction in Cincinnati for the violation of Ohio's Equal Rights Law was handed down against a restaurant.

Several intergroup agencies and various private associations are an important part of the human relations picture in Cincinnati, and their work during the 1940's was indicative of the changing emphasis in this field. The Mayor's Friendly Relations Committee, the National Conference of Christians and Jews, Urban League, the National Association for the

Advancement of Colored People (NAACP), Fellowship House, the interracial work of some of the churches, the YWCA and the Girl Scouts (and to a lesser degree the YMCA and the Boy Scouts) have helped create the environment in which non-segregated patterns could be worked out. The number of such agencies and the variety of their programs show that in this respect Cincinnati is a Northern city, giving more active support to intergroup agencies than has been possible in the past in most Southern cities. Their leadership has done much to relieve tensions and remove irritants to both races.

Since World War II the downtown theaters, restaurants, and hotels have opened their doors to Negroes. Economic pressure from convention groups having bi-racial personnel was important in these cases, as well as the educational activities of the interracial agencies. However, many Negroes still feel a good deal of uncertainty about being served without embarrassment in some of the restaurants. Segregation practices in public parks and swimming pools have been sharply curtailed in the last few years. Initial tension and some boycotting by whites did not lead to any violence, and both the tension and the boycotting declined within a reasonably short time. Residential segregation tends to limit use of non-segregated public facilities, however.

Did this steady movement in the human relations pattern come about because the Negro was only a small proportion of the total population? The answer seems to be, not at all. Both the central city and the metropolitan area grew rapidly during the past decade, the population of the city increasing 10 per cent and the metropolitan area almost 15 per cent. Much of the increase was accounted for by Negro and white workers from Kentucky, West Virginia, Tennessee, and Alabama who might be expected to reflect intransigent attitudes on race questions. Between 1940 and 1950 the white population grew by 6 per cent while the Negro population increased 41 per cent. In 1950 the Negro represented almost 16 per cent of the city's total, or one-sixth of the half-million residents; because of the smaller Negro settlements in the suburbs, only about 11 per cent of the metropolitan area is Negro. The proportional increase in the Negro population should be kept in mind, for it seems to contradict the usual assertions that as a minority becomes more numerous and hence visible, it attracts or generates more friction or adverse criticism. It remains possible, of course, that this conflict-potential may have been created only to be cancelled by other forces.

The major facts of residential segregation, unequal opportunities, and prejudice remain, but an acceleration of change is apparent. The Negro residential pattern is similar to many other cities: a large, over-crowded section in the heart of the city, much of it slum, housing approximately 40 per cent of the Negroes; and some small scattered settlements in other parts of the city. Isolated Negro households in predominantly white neighborhoods are unusual. Insofar as this total pattern is changing, it is by the reduction of the proportion of Negroes living in the central area and an increase in the number of smaller islands. The decisions of the school authorities on improvement of facilities reflects this population mobility.

In job opportunities and income the Negro is at a marked disadvantage. In 1949 the median income for Negro families or single individuals was $1,645, while the median for whites was $2,970. In 1950, 87 per cent of the Negro labor force was employed, compared with almost 96 per cent of the white. In the Cincinnati office of the Ohio State Employment Service, 76 per cent of all job orders filled or cancelled in a ten week period in 1952 specified "for white only." These employment restrictions relate to past discrimination in schooling (when Negroes possessed few of the requisite skills for technical jobs) as well as to continuing prejudice. On the other hand, some firms are now hiring Negro stenographers; the General Hospital has accepted two Negro interns, and another hospital has Negroes at almost every level of its staff. More Negro teachers have been hired in recent years. Although direct evidence is not available, these developments may mean that some important opportunities for advancement for Negroes have come first at the white collar and professional level, where education and common interests and activities may have reduced prejudice, rather than in the semi-skilled and skilled trades where both prejudice and fear of competition have been more marked—in spite of the emphasis on trade or technical schools for the less privileged.

Schools strongly reflect the residential pattern of a community, and residence in turn reflects income and job opportunities, recreational choices, and other institutional facts. Shifts in administrative policies are inevitably limited by—and yet in turn affect—other forces at work in the community. The direction of change in Cincinnati has been clear since the early 1940's; but the pace has been slow. In addition to the work done by the interracial agencies, individual Negro parents and principals and teachers continually asked for more complete school integration. The school administration favored the policy, and it was not hampered by negativism on the school board. The redirection of the school system was brought about with virtually no publicity, no influence from the state board of education or the state political situation, and with a minimum of difficulty.

As a background for presenting the present school picture, some complicating factors should be kept in mind. There are several private elementary schools within the city attended primarily by white children. A smaller proportion of Negroes finish high school than do white children, a generalization applicable to each of the communities studied. The net effect is to increase the proportion of Negro children in the lower grades in Cincinnati. Most children attend school at least through the sixth grade; after that a decline is apparent, particularly among Negroes. The 1950 census reports that in Cincinnati the median number of years in school completed by white persons twenty-five years of age or more is two to three more than by Negroes in the same age group. Only about 40 per cent of the white students in the seventh grade in 1946 were in the twelfth grade in the spring of 1951. The corresponding figure for the Negro class was 16 per cent, representing a drop of 84 per cent for this class. The drop-out rate between 1947 and 1952 was 54 per cent for white students and 75 per cent for Negroes. How much this reflects economic pressure and how much it is an index of less encouragement for Negroes to continue in school is not known.

The number of schools with some Negro pupils is increasing slowly. This is not a function of changed policy but of a wider distribution of Negro settlements outside the Basin. Fifty-nine of the eighty-three public schools now have a biracial student body. There is also a slow increase in the proportion of Negro pupils attending schools that are not completely or overwhelmingly Negro. As of 1953 this would include between 10 and 15 per cent of the Negro pupils. Residential segregation results in the fact that between 85 and 90 per cent of the Negro pupils are in schools where the student body is predominantly (75 per cent or more) or completely Negro.

The status of the three segregated schools in the Basin has changed officially; they were districted in the fall of 1953. On the surface this would seem to be a move in the direction of segregation since only Negroes now live in the districts. However, some Negro teachers themselves regard it as a gain, because any white children who may come to live in the district will be assigned to these schools. If the fourth segregated school in Walnut Hills is districted in 1954 as has been suggested, it will be a definite move toward integration, for this school is located in an area which is almost evenly divided in numbers of Negro and white.

In the integrated schools, formal and informal segregation has decreased markedly since 1950. Cincinnati schools have withdrawn from athletic contests with schools which would not compete against a bi-racial team. The clearest change was in swimming, which until 1950 was both compulsory and segregated in all high schools. After consultation with the Mayor's Friendly Relations Committee and other groups, the school officials announced a new policy: swimming was to be voluntary and integrated. There was an abrupt drop in the size of classes, ranging from 45 to nearly 90 per cent in the various schools. Much of this was due simply to a desire to avoid swimming. Doctor's excuses had been fairly common in the past. Some, evidently, was obvious unwillingness to accept the integrated pattern. By 1953, after skillful work by teachers and interracial groups, the average enrollments ranged from 41 to 90 per cent of the pupils in the various schools.

Other developments represented steps toward integrated faculties. About 1940 the superintendent brought Negroes into a committee concerned with the problems of children and schools throughout the city. The Upper Grades Study Council already had Negroes on its board. The administration encouraged teachers to attend interracial workshops, starting about 1943. At that time, also, some Negro men teachers were admitted to the Schoolmasters' Club; the former all-Negro Schoolmens' Club is gradually going out of existence. These specific and accumulating experiences helped pave the way for smooth transition to integrated faculties.

The first step toward integration of faculties was made in 1944. The school administration was convinced that integration was just and necessary. There was some feeling, for example, that children of either race were more inclined to be tense and insecure when they were treated as a minority group by teachers not of their own race. The superintendent of schools was the first chairman of the Mayor's Friendly Relations Committee, and an assistant superintendent had sponsored interracial committees of teachers and attendance at the interracial workshops. He was directly involved in the establishment of the first integrated faculty in a school where almost all the students were Negro. The few white pupils were transferred to other schools in the belief that it would be better to integrate at only one level at a time although these children were already accustomed to being a minority in the student body.

Members of the all-white faculty at first expressed a good deal of opposition to accepting Negro colleagues. The principal talked with each individual, persuaded several to try the experiment, and then told the rest that they would be transferred to other schools if they preferred. Most of them decided to stay, and the change went through without obvious tension or difficulty. In 1948 an integrated faculty was started in a school where about 20 per cent of the pupils were white. For the first time in Cincinnati, Negro teachers had white pupils in their classes. This move was prefaced by consultations with parents. The change was explained, and most parents who were consulted accepted it. Some objected individually, but there was no organized move to discredit the arrangement.

By 1953 five elementary and two junior high schools had integrated faculties, usually with about equal proportions of white and Negro teachers. There was one Negro principal of an integrated school, one assistant principal, and a few counsellors and deans. Since about 1944 the number of Negro teachers has increased from about 150 to 200. That this is not the end of the process is shown by the fact that by the 1953-1954 school year, the integrated faculties as yet were found only in schools where the student body was preponderantly Negro. There were no Negroes on high school faculties although this was being considered for the fall of 1954. Should this change occur, it will be interesting to see if more Negro students complete high school. As will be shown in another study reported in this work, the integration of high school faculties in some communities apparently decreased tensions and facilitated student adjustments at that level.

What were some of the reactions to integration? Within the student bodies integration was not new, technically, since there had been many unsegregated schools for years. The only new development was an increase in the number of children involved. The main innovation was the establishment of the integrated faculties. This had been initiated only after careful study and planning by the school administration, consultations with the teachers involved, and with parents in instances where this was felt necessary. No organized opposition to the move developed although it was well known that some individuals, both faculty and parents, found it distasteful. The Negro teachers greeted it as "a breath of fresh air," a relief from anxiety, and an encouragement to better teaching. Here there was no attempt to protect segregated schools as a source of employment, a reaction found fairly frequently when the dual system has been unequally endowed or where the Negro teacher is in a noncompetitive position with the white.

Most white teachers were not affected by the innovation. Of those who were, a few disapproved and accepted assignments in other schools; most accepted the change, and some actively supported and participated in it. Skillful administration, a minimum of publicity, the careful choice of principals and Negro teachers, teacher training in intergroup relations, and talks to the students on the subject were the major means used in trying to keep difficulties at a minimum. There is some evidence that within the school situation rowdiness and disciplinary problems were reduced. There was no evidence, however, that friendship patterns or group membership outside the school had been greatly affected. These remain for the most part, as before, socially distinct and segregated.

Originally some Negro parents objected to the move on the grounds that their children would have less sympathetic understanding and help from white teachers. Most were enthusiastic, however, and helped to bring the change about. Some informed local observers have predicted that Negro children might stay in school longer since they feel that opportunities to use a better education are greater than ever before. The most important fact about white parents' acceptance is that they *have* accepted Negro teachers even though many of them are prejudiced and would prefer a segregated school. One white mother, brought up in West Virginia, said that when she first moved to Cincinnati she wanted to go home rather than send her children to an integrated school. But she sent them, found that no difficulties arose, and saw that they liked their school very much. When Negro teachers came, she felt no reason to object, and her children liked them all. At the same time this parent did not want her children to eat in the cafeteria at school or play with Negro students off the school grounds. She became perfectly tolerant about the school situation but otherwise did not change her attitudes very much. That this mixture of attitudes can occur in such circumstances, without occasioning problems so far as the school system is concerned, is an important fact in considering the possibilities and the consequences of school desegregation. Where the total environment operates in mutually exclusive social patterns but is not actively hostile to well-defined and limited patterns of change, desegregation of schools can be instituted with a minimum of friction.

Teachers and administrators were unanimous in declaring that white children accepted Negro teachers without difficulty and often with enthusiasm. There may be a tendency to underestimate the tension which some white children felt as a result of being a small minority (1 or 2 to 25 per cent) in schools predominantly Negro where the integrated faculties were initiated. With regard to this factor, there is some suggestion that it might be easier to place Negro teachers in schools predominantly white. Many of the Negro children were keenly aware of the innovation and favorably disposed toward it. A principal who had worked with the process from the beginning said that tension level as shown by fights and name-calling on the playground had been reduced significantly. The Negro children felt more secure, more self-confident, and better motivated.

The experience of Cincinnati may be summed up by listing some of its advantages and some of the obstacles it faced.

There was state legal support for integration, and there was a local tradition of some integrated student bodies. The upper socioeconomic classes were tolerant and to some degree active in supporting bi-racial harmony. The school officials, and the Mayor's Friendly Relations Committee with its trained staff, continuously looked for ways to reduce interracial tensions. A number of private interracial agencies were also alert to the educational situation.

On the other hand Cincinnati has some important characteristics in common with Southern cities: a large, mostly lower-income class Negro population; a high proportion of Southern people, both white and Negro; employment and residential patterns imposing limitations on the shift toward greater integration. It is generally regarded as a conservative city, making changes deliberately and after long thought.

A striking fact about the process of integration is the gradual increase of interracial activity *before* any considerable movement toward integration had begun. From the time Negroes were brought into a committee concerned with the schools and children (1940), it was four years before there was an integrated public school faculty, and eight years before the appearance of an integrated faculty in a school with a sizeable proportion of white pupils. It was a decade before there were major breaches in the walls of segregation *within* the schools having pupils of both races. As of 1953— some fifteen years after the first salient symptoms of change— the city is just planning for the first Negro teachers in the high schools.

On the whole the movement of this process has been toward integration. It has not happened by massive steps, but by a change here and a change there. The various adjustments have occurred quietly and without major crises.

The legal framework within which an integrated school system could develop was available for many years before the local mores and customs changed to permit such a move. Nor could the change have been made without the thoughtful planning and firm policies advanced by the superintendent of schools and his staff. A recurrent theme in all the communities studied is the essential role played by the school officials; where they were in a real sense community leaders, potential disturbances seldom developed. Wavering and fearful school administrators were unable to control either the school situation or community reaction to it. This does not mean that all prejudice evaporated in the well-managed communities. Far from it. But the evidence seems clear that cooperative planning which recognizes established feelings can reduce actual discriminations long before it is possible to remove deep-rooted prejudice.

CHAPTER 4

Variation Under the Law:
INDIANAPOLIS AND OTHER INDIANA COMMUNITIES *

THIS CHAPTER FOCUSES ON THE STATE OF INDIANA—A KEYSTONE area connecting Middle West and South. Major interest here attaches to the case study of the metropolitan center of Indianapolis, a city where industrial patterns combine with rural heritage, where one can walk through areas in which the voices heard carry the familiar accents of Kentucky, Tennessee, and points east and south. Along with the example of Indianapolis will be seen something of how movement toward integration has affected a number of other Indiana communities, smaller in size but no less important in illuminating some basic American problems.

Particularly worth attention in this review of experience in Indiana are the illustrations of the influence of uncertainty as to community sentiments upon the actions of school authorities. Here are examples of how new action toward integration has faltered before the belief that community acceptance is less than later events demonstrate to be the case. There are instances that show in full-life proportions the need for two-way channels of communication, for care-

* Based on the report of field research prepared by Harold T. Christensen, Dwight W. Culver, Purdue University; and John Gandy, Assistant Research Director of the Welfare Council of Metropolitan Chicago.

ful preparation of both faculty and parents, and for continuing civic bodies concerned with human relations. The evidence is that once the school policy has been accepted, the
school itself can function solely as an educational institution,
leaving many of the broader and marginal problems of
general community concern to other agencies.

Indianapolis

From 1877 to 1949 local school boards in Indiana could
decide whether the elementary, the secondary schools, both
or neither were to be segregated. All possible combinations
were tried in different parts of the state. Indianapolis had
integrated schools until, during the 1920's, the power of the
Ku Klux Klan forced many of the Negro children into segregated schools. Having its headquarters in the city, under
Grand Dragon D. S. Stephenson, the Klan secured the erection of Crispus Attucks High School in 1927 and established
it as a segregated school. In the same year a Klan-dominated
school board initiated the policy of transporting Negroes
away from the elementary school in their neighborhood to
more distant schools for Negroes. By 1947, out of a total of
eighty-one public elementary schools, fourteen were for
Negroes, fifty-nine were for whites, and eight were integrated.

A document sent by the Board of School Commissioners to
the Education Committee of the House of Representatives in
1947 stated in part:

Since 1875 the City of Indianapolis through its Boards of School
Commissioners has followed the general, but not absolute, policy
of providing separate schools for Negroes. The legality of such
procedure has been tested and upheld several times by court
decisions. The law gives the Board of School Commissioners
broad powers in establishing and maintaining its schools, and for
"districting and dividing the city for school purposes."

At present 14 elementary schools and one high school are being maintained for Negro pupils. These schools represent a capital investment of $3,233,812.00. In these schools there are 9,305 Negro pupils and 366 Negro employees, including 215 elementary teachers, 14 elementary school principals, 3 assistant principals, one assistant high school principal, 14 high school department heads, and 47 custodians, janitors and matrons. Many of these teachers are entitled to indefinite contracts under the teacher tenure law of Indiana. There are ten elementary schools in which both Negro and white pupils are enrolled. In the past, as at present, when shifts in population have occurred, the Commissioners have had to consider such practical matters as available building facilities and feasibility of transportation of pupils in determining which schools they shall attend.

This statement represented the board's views in 1949, when the new anti-segregation law was being debated in the legislature. It carries the strong implicit appeal to considerations of established practice, to vested interests in capital and jobs, to administrative rigidities. It stresses the sheer "mechanical" difficulty of adjustments to change in a large-scale school system. Such considerations are likely to bulk large in the minds of educational administrators whenever any major change in established practice is contemplated.

After the defeat of an integration bill in the Indiana General Assembly in 1947, a campaign against segregation was conducted by Negro and interracial organizations and by church groups in the city. Three of the positions on the school board were contested by candidates who were in opposition on the issue of segregation. Since it was customary for the Citizens' School Committee to put up a single slate which was rarely opposed, this focused attention on the issue. Negro members of the Citizens' School Committee had tried unsuccessfully to nominate a Negro to the board and had suggested that a more democratic election procedure would speed the desegregation process.

In May, 1948, after a two-hour session of speeches by a delegation of 40 Negro and white persons, with petitions signed by 950 persons representing individuals and organizations in support of the proposals, the commissioners took under advisement a proposal to: 1) Allow all elementary school children regardless of race to go to the school within their district; 2) Allow all high school students, regardless of race, to attend a school of their choice. The representative of the NAACP who presented the proposal said that he would return to the next board meeting to learn whether a decision had been reached. When nothing further was heard from the board on this subject, the city and state officials of the NAACP gave the school board a thirty-day deadline for a statement of intention on the continuance of the segregation policy. A document presented by NAACP to the board said in part, "We are ready and willing to help our School Commissioners to initiate a policy of democratic educational opportunities *at once. . . .*" The board made no reply. The NAACP announced in October, 1948, its intention to file an injunction suit in the Indianapolis Federal Court to force the Board of School Commissioners to abolish racial segregation. The announcement contained the statement that "Citizens of various races and religions appeared before the present school board four times this year and made protests as to its policy, and presented them with a practical blue print for an integrated program over a period of three years beginning in January, 1949. . . ."

At its next meeting the board split on whether to make a public statement or wait for the suit to be filed. In December the NAACP announced that it would refrain from taking further action until the results of the fact-finding survey to be made by the Indianapolis Community Relations Council was completed late in the spring. If no program for abolishing segregation was begun after the survey findings were made available to the commissioners, the injunction suit would be filed.

Some findings of a pilot survey made by a representative of the National Community Relations Advisory Council in May, 1948, are relevant here. The pilot study showed that since the Free Kindergarten Society operated twenty-seven non-segregated kindergartens, parents reported some difficulty explaining to beginning first-graders why they could not attend school with children with whom they had played in kindergarten. Another finding was that "Teachers agree that there have never been any serious disturbances because of racial differences either in the schools which have always been non-segregated or in previously segregated schools which recently opened their doors to Negro children in the neighborhood."

In the fall of 1948 the first disturbance over the integration of a school called attention to the attitudes of parents toward the practice of selecting certain schools for beginning the process. White children were withdrawn from School No. 32 where Negro children were admitted for the first time to the first six grades. Some of the parents of the almost 200 white pupils who boycotted the school made it clear that their protest was aimed at the board rather than at the Negroes. They knew that the board had refused to open School No. 43 to Negroes although it had two library rooms which could have been converted to class rooms. A typical comment was, "We think the Board should be fair about it, that's all. If they're going to end segregation, they should end it all over and not just pick out one certain school for mixing white and Negro children." Another said, "We don't object to our children going to school with Negro kids. It's just that we don't like to be pushed around by those north-side swells. If they don't like to take in the Negro children at School No. 43, why should we?" The boycotting was short-lived, but the issue was stated clearly. One mother expressed the group attitude when she said that she would keep her children away from school until the board decided one way or another on segregation.

The board denied that the change in school assignment had anything to do with race; they contended that they were concerned only with equal educational opportunities for all children in the city. However, the lack of a definite stand by the board on the question of segregation brought opposition from Negroes to the board's plans to take over twenty-seven kindergartens from the Indianapolis Free Kindergarten Society and expand the system to cover all five-year olds in the city. The stand taken by leading Negroes was that this should not be done "unless the Board adopts a non-discrimination policy." The basic fact here was that the society kindergartens had not been segregated. Opposition was registered also to plans for a shop addition to Attucks High School, on the grounds that the plan was "an admission that the facilities at Attucks are not equal to those of the six other high schools. . . ." The survey for which NAACP had been deferring its legal action was abandoned when the board refused to approve it. Without this approval, research personnel from Indiana University could not participate. By this time, said a former board member, the board had become aware of the strength of community attitudes favoring desegregation and was making plans for a gradual program.

All the organizations which had been bringing pressure upon the school commissioners now turned their attention to the Indiana General Assembly, and when the State anti-segregation law was passed in March, 1949 [1] they continued their efforts at home to achieve an integrated school system.

Newspaper editorials at the time were forthright in their support of the desegregated school. One article stated that the school authorities admitted privately that the new law pushed them toward integration a little faster than they

1. See Chapter 2, pp. 25-26; also Appendix II.

wanted to go, but that they thought that the reaction of the community would not be as marked as some of the supporters of segregation predicted. The real protest, they felt, would come from the integration of faculties, not of student bodies. That a protest based on this point was audible in only one section of the city will be discussed below.

From the changed perspective of U.S.A., 1954, much of this might seem a tempest in a tea pot, since most of the Negro population (16 per cent of the total population of over 425,000 in 1950) was confined by unofficial real estate agreements and economic factors to specific sections north-west and north-east of the city center, roughly the Negro high school district. Nevertheless, strong resistances to integration had been aroused.

At the time the anti-segregation law was being considered by the state legislature, two North Side civic leagues demanded its defeat, taking particular issue with a section which provided for "hiring, upgrading, tenure, or placement of any teacher" without consideration of race, color, or creed. It was contended that this section of the bill was harmful since it provided for "placement of teachers of one race in schools entirely or largely composed of students of another race." That the protests came from the middle- and upper-class neighborhoods, shortly after a school strike in a lower middle-class area, seemed to bear out the contention of the parents in the latter area that desegregation was not being pursued as a city-wide policy. The piecemeal approach suddenly appeared not as a gradual solution but as a factor creating neighborhood distinctions, dissatisfactions, and antipathy to the board's decisions.

The new state law was held constitutional by the attorney general—but with the advice to the governor that "as it now stands, the act makes nothing unlawful and carries no penal provisions." The NAACP announced immediately that it would invoke a writ of mandamus, if necessary, to secure compliance with the law. The gradual desegregation permitted under the law, however, left much individual initiative to the local boards in their application of the law and in their interpretation of the speed with which it could be applied in each community.

A specific and vital problem facing the Indianapolis School Board at that time was the districting of the high schools. On April 12, 1949, the superintendent submitted a plan in compliance with the law. It applied to school children who were entering, in September, 1949, 1) the first semester of the elementary schools; 2) the first semester of the high school; and 3) kindergarten. By a new interpretation, junior high schools were considered to be *elementary* schools and would not receive their first integrated classes until 1955— rather than in 1951 as would have been required by law had they been considered separately. Assignment of approximately 2,500 pupils in grade 8A to high schools was made on the basis of previous registrations in the particular high school from each elementary school district; but for the first time distance from the pupil's residence to the assigned school was considered indirectly. The new policy permitted transfers, if requested, in the beginning high school assignments if the pupil lived more than two miles from the designated school and less than two miles from another. Transfer requests were also considered from pupils living more than two miles from any high school or if they presented another justifiable reason. Skeptical critics might say that this last phrase left the way open to avoid desegregated schools. Nevertheless, approximately 200 Negro freshmen entered high schools previously for whites in the first application of the policy.

This policy statement provided that in so far as facilities were available, the 5,000 elementary beginners in September, 1949, were to be assigned to the public school nearest their residence. For such beginners only, the boundaries of the school districts might be modified in certain instances. Changes in assignment for entering beginners were to be considered if the pupil lived more than one mile from any public elementary school and was not provided transportation or if he presented some other justifiable reason which had usually been regarded in the past as a basis for transfer. These statements were unclear to many people, who were puzzled as to the exact intent of the school authorities in such cases. It was clear, however, that all other pupils then enrolled in the public schools were to continue to attend the same schools subject to the previous rules and procedures covering transfers.

This plan was the minimum permitted by law, and although the two- and one-mile circles delineated by board action were a rough approximation of districts they allegedly were the basis for *permitting transfers*, not for *making assignments*. The board was accused of hedging, of leaving decisions as to what school district a child lived in up to the individual parents. The *Indianapolis Recorder*, a Negro newspaper, commented in part, "Under such a cynical plan, some Negro parents would have to take their children to a hitherto 'white' school without having a clear, public recognition of their right to do so.... The failure to inform the public in unmistakable terms of the boundaries of all the school districts, creates doubt and confusion about the law, and provides a breeding-ground for agitation by hate-minded persons." [2] Not until August, 1953, were elementary and high school district maps available to all principals and interested parties. The two- and one-mile circles were distorted by topography and transportation features for the high school districts, and the four "optional" districts involving Attucks High School seemed to be definitely more related to the Negro residential areas than to a boundary circle based on distance, since another adjacent optional district, where the

2. *Indianapolis Recorder*, August 20, 1949.

choice was either of two schools formerly for whites, was a white neighborhood. This new policy represented a move toward integration, but it still permitted a mixed arrangement in which the boundaries of districts could not be defined solely in terms of nearness to school. A sidelight on the freedom in school administration enjoyed by the board is that, although many civic organizations rallied to the support of the anti-segregation bill before it became law, their support and interest subsided and most of them were not heard from again. This made it possible for the board to have a relatively free hand in determining policy, for the school principals to act somewhat independently, and for both levels of administration to move slowly and conservatively in making changes.

By 1953 the process of desegregation had been completed in the high schools, and the first integrated classes, which had entered the schools previously for whites in 1949, were graduated. The proportion of Negroes in the different schools ranged up to 13 per cent of the total student body, although most high schools had no more than 6 to 8 per cent. At the elementary school level, desegregation was completed through the fourth grade, and these children were starting the fifth grade. As of October, 1953, forty-seven elementary schools enrolled both Negro and white pupils. Forty-three of these had a Negro minority and four had a white minority. Twenty-seven schools enrolled only Negroes. These schools were in residentially segregated neighborhoods.

No one connected with the schools denied that Attucks High School remained for Negroes only or that the policy of the board was to keep it that way. However, children who lived outside the two major centers of Negro concentration were assigned to the high schools which were predominantly white and were allowed to transfer to Crispus Attucks only for special reasons. Those in the concentrated Negro areas were usually enrolled at Attucks, even though alternatives were offered in the optional districts adjoining.

A drop in the enrollment at Attucks was partly a result of desegregation inasmuch as no whites made up the loss of Negro students. The June total dropped from 2,364 in 1949 to 1,612 in 1953. A slight increase was expected in the fall of 1953 as a result of increased Negro choice of Attucks rather than the desegregated schools. The decline in Attucks enrollment was taken advantage of indirectly to relieve the pressure on the elementary schools for Negroes. There were 500 pupils in the seventh and eighth grades at Attucks, making it in effect a six-year high school. The controversial addition to the shop facilities previously noted was dedicated just a few months after the anti-segregation law was passed, and it was said to have resulted in the Negro students getting a much better shop training than was possible at any other high school in the city. There was a smaller enrollment at Attucks and thus a better chance for training with the tools and for personal instruction. It is believed in Indianapolis that the intention of school authorities is to keep Attucks as a Negro service institution apart from the integrated system.

During the four-year period of transition (1949-1953) to definite school districts, the procedures for transfers were made increasingly specific, and it was stated explicity that no transfers were to be made by reason of race, color, or religion. The cards on which applications for transfer are now made at the high school level do not include any reference to race.

A weaker link in the chain from policy to practice was the elementary school transfers, which were handled by the principals concerned. One Negro principal, interviewed in August, 1953, did not know that it was necessary for him to approve the transfer of white children out of the district in which his segregated school was located. He thought, "If they are white, all they have to do is to go to the white principal of the other school." No procedure had been established to insure that elementary school transfers were reported by the principals. There were indications that in the future, district lines would be adhered to more firmly in assigning children, especially when applications for transfers were brought to the attention of the school administration. However, this still put the burden of decision on the parents.

In several cases pressure of enrollment on the school facilities made it necessary to speed up the desegregation timetable. To relieve over-crowding in one school for Negroes, about 125 children were moved in 1953 to a school previously for whites. The Negro principal explained the decision to the PTA and made it clear that any parents who objected would not have to agree to sending their children. The board sent letters to all parents whose children were to be transferred explaining the reason, and they were moved without incident. Advance preparation and explanation were essential parts of the smooth transfer.

Faculty integration in Indianapolis did not begin until 1951. In the mid-1940's a committee of Negro and white principals had been active in the consideration of the problems involved in desegregation. During this time, a list of Negro teachers who could be used in the new program was compiled, taking into consideration such characteristics as grasp of subject matter, ability to teach, and personal neatness. Plans to introduce Negro teachers into schools for whites and white teachers into schools for Negroes at about the same time had been talked of, but some informed persons claimed that pressure from the NAACP and the Negro newspaper made it necessary to place a few Negro teachers in the non-segregated schools before two-way transfer could be arranged. No official statement had been made with regard to using white teachers in the schools for Negroes. The current policy was to assign only Negro teachers to the schools for Negroes, white teachers to schools for whites, white teachers to the desegregated high schools, and an occasional Negro to the desegregated elementary schools.

There was still a definite ceiling on the number of Negro teachers who could be employed, and certain jobs seemed to be earmarked clearly either for Negro or white teachers. Five Negro teachers and one Negro principal were assigned to three integrated schools (out of forty-seven such schools), and some other Negroes rendered special services in the desegregated schools. An analysis of the lists of new teachers employed each year showed a lower rate of turn-over and new employment for Negroes than for whites. One school official said that if it were possible to hire new teachers without regard to race, the problem of filling vacancies would be much easier. In the past all Negroes assigned to the desegregated schools had been in the system for some time, and these assignments did not increase the total number of Negro teachers in the system. In September, 1951, 6 out of 165 new teachers were Negro; in 1953 there were 5 out of 265 new teachers. According to some Indianapolis people, it was thought possible that the low representation of the minority group at the faculty level in the desegregated schools might account in part for the relatively poorer adjustment patterns of Negro students there.

That there is no one "right" way to look at an integration process will be seen by the variety of responses the interviewers encountered in the course of the study. There was no evidence that the teachers at Attucks were attempting to keep Negro students there or that they felt insecure about their jobs under integration. One official reported that when students wished to transfer back to Attucks, an interview was held with their parents, who had to justify the transfers on some basis other than race. He did note a tendency in the desegregated schools to confuse problems of discipline in the case of the Negro pupils with "lack of intelligence" and said that he watched carefully for any attempt to classify Negroes as "special" students to facilitate their transfer back to Attucks, which already had 250 special students at the high school level. Attucks has a strong reclassification program, accounting in part for the large number of special students. One of the vocational advisers in an optional high school district said that he recommended Attucks only to those students who were slow learners and that his students who had chosen the desegregated schools had done well.

Another administrator thought that the number of students choosing Attucks was influenced primarily by transportation facilities and by the appeal of extra-curricular activities (especially baseball), rather than by the treatment accorded them in the other schools. Students from one elementary school in the Attucks district, and the one most distant from the high school, chose that school, thirty-one to seven, over the desegregated Technical High School in 1953. They were on a bus line which took them all the way to Attucks without a transfer. Another elementary school, nearer to both Attucks and Technical, is within walking distance of the latter, and students in grade 8A this same year divided almost evenly, forty-two for Attucks and forty for Technical.

When they were asked to evaluate the program, Negro students in the desegregated schools placed considerable emphasis on the attitudes of white faculty and students toward Negroes. A girl who attended a desegregated school for one year asked for a transfer back to Attucks. Her desire was not prompted by any one incident but by the fact that the general atmosphere at school was not comfortable. There were no major interracial incidents, but she felt that some teachers were prejudiced and that there was a lack of correction of white students making fun of Negroes in the classroom. At Attucks the girl was an outstanding student. The girl's mother thought that the antagonism at the school reflected the section of the city in which it was located. The area around the school is one in which the Ku Klux Klan was strong at one time and in which Negroes were still refused admission to theaters and fountain service in drug stores.

On the other hand, some of the administrators in this school thought that the students who were unhappy in the integrated situation would be just as unhappy at Attucks. Some said that Negroes tended to be noisier than whites although these persons recognized that this was a reaction to, as well as a cause of, prejudice on the part of white teachers and students. They also believed that Negro students tended to segregate themselves within the school and that the issue of discrimination was raised when discipline was needed. This was a school in which Negroes had no part in extra-curricular activities. Thus, Negro students felt discrimination, but administrative officers appeared to be quite unaware of this. The fact that the channels of communication between students, teachers, and the administration were not clearly defined made possible such diverse views of the same school situation.

A social studies teacher at another high school was thought to get along better with her Negro students than did some of her colleagues because she told her classes, "I reserve the right to dislike what you are doing regardless of your race or religion!" She expressed the opinion that impartial discipline could be employed with Negro students, without discrimination, and that they would like it. Specifically, she said that noisy children of any group could be brought to more acceptable behavior if the correct approach was used. She thought also that most white teachers were prejudiced against Negro students, in spite of their denials. In one instance a white girl and a Negro boy were walking down the hall discussing plans for a program in which they both were to appear. A teacher drew the girl aside and asked loudly enough for the boy to hear, "Are you a *Negro?*" This incident was immediately known all over the senior class; most of the students and the teachers sympathized with the two students in this instance. In this school there was integration in sports, the choir and band, and in other activities.

The school with the highest proportion of Negroes—16 per cent—had the most serious adjustment problems. The administration knew that there were cases of teacher prejudice and discrimination in spite of a policy which was non-discriminatory. Negro students reported that the instances of teacher prejudice were well known to all the Negroes there; one said that some of the teachers gave the Negro "a rough time" because of his color but that the majority were fair. Negro students felt that they were discriminated against in grading, that borderline grades were settled lower for them, and that discretion in the evaluation of absences seldom favored them. They did not feel welcome to participate in extra-curricular activities. Yet, the same students who reported these things thought that the principal and his administrative staff were so liberal that the integration program could be considered a success.

Even though Negro teachers did not feel insecure under the program, there was some bitterness expressed at what one called making every Negro appointment a "production." A number of Negro teachers had declined appointments in integrated schools, because they were opposed to the idea of the white teachers being asked whether or not they wanted to work with Negroes. They would have preferred that all teachers be assigned on the same basis without solicitude for the feelings of the whites alone. It appeared that the top-level administration rather than the principals was blamed for the policy. One administrator was quoted as saying, "We won't need Negro teachers now, because the Negroes are going to the white schools." Another was alleged to have refused to appoint a Negro teacher to an integrated school after the principal had requested one to help with his problems of discipline.

These allegations of undercurrents of resentment may indicate one basis of the lack of enthusiasm with which the appointment of a Negro woman as principal of an integrated school was hailed when it was announced in August, 1953. In this position she supervised three Negro and five white teachers, all carefully selected and prepared for the new experience. Some said that the school board would point to this as evidence of faculty integration and go no further, at least for several years. Others suggested that the appointment was a reward for the new principal's testimony in the suit against the school board earlier in the year. Whether or not jealousy was involved, the resentment appeared to have been directed at the school board, rather than at any of the administrators under its authority.

Here again, it is obvious that communities have histories which people remember. The case which this appointment recalled was one involving a protest against the time-table of integration, in the form of a suit against the school board, after the request for transfer of some Negro children into the fifth and sixth grades at a school for whites had been denied. Following a full day of testimony, delay in a continued hearing, and a mandate from the State Supreme Court, a rehearing was scheduled. The superintendent denied that there was inequality between the two schools concerned; he testified that the order to enroll the children at the school for Negroes was made because they were part of a group of twenty-six children completing the fourth grade in June, 1952, who were transferred as a group to another such school. "It is the general School Board policy to transfer pupils who have been associated together for a time in a group to another school when necessary. It's good psychology and good economics." The plaintiffs indicated by their line of questioning that the proposed erection of a new school, No. 64, at a cost of $750,000 would be necessary only if segregation was to be continued. The court ruled that "equality of facilities does not exist" but held that "the Board of School Commissioners has authority to create districts, and that such school districts may overlap other districts, or go beyond the boundaries of adjoining school districts because of the existing school districts, availability of facilities, and overcrowding of certain schools." The court indicated that the board had complied with the law and also that the school to which the Negro parent wished to send his children did not have sufficient space to accommodate all the students. The court, therefore, found that the board was doing its duty in this case. It is said that the Negro community did not support the plaintiff in the case, and this strengthened the conviction of the school administration that they were proceeding as quickly as necessary in the integration program.

The publicity given the appointment of the Negro principal represented a departure from one of the policies of the Indianapolis Board of Education. The board had maintained a "no publicity" policy from the beginning of the desegregation process. It is reported that when the faculty integration was begun, they called in the newspapers and requested that nothing be reported on the progress in this phase. Since 1950, the present administration had had meetings with students, teachers, and with PTA's, and it had conducted surveys to determine community sentiment in the affected areas; all this they are said to have tried to do without press comment.

That this is a feat difficult to accomplish is shown by a file of clippings from 1947 to 1953, involving more than 130 news stories, editorials, and letters. All editorials approved the ending of segregation, and all news stories presented the actions of the board in a favorable light, except in the period of indecision before the passage of the state law. On the basis of what was printed, some informants in the community could not understand why the board had not released fuller information to the press. Informants said that the community did not have the tradition of demanding information from its school officials and that the principals guarded their jurisdiction carefully.

There was evidence that within the school system the flow

of communication was partly blocked in an upward direction. Because of this, some of the things which the administrators needed to know (especially about the attitudes and feelings of teachers and students in relation to each other) were not reported to them. Tensions and misunderstandings thus tended to go unchecked; teachers who were known to be openly prejudiced went undisciplined. The board had no direct way of knowing by tangible evidence whether a program of in-group training in interracial relations was needed. One member thought that no mistakes had been made. A directing official in the public school system thought that they might have moved a little faster, but not much faster without arousing antagonism and opposition. His view perhaps adequately suggests the atmosphere in which the Indianapolis story of desegregation has unfolded.

The Smaller Indiana Cities

None of these communities will be discussed in such detail as have been Cincinnati and Indianapolis. They will be used instead to illustrate and pin-point some of the specific configurations encountered in changing a community pattern. In general these cities have grown rapidly in the last decade, but not so rapidly as the Negro population in them has increased. Because of restriction of Negro homes to certain areas of the cities, this growth has led to increased density in the residential areas occupied by Negroes. The period of recent changes has been a prosperous era, and, partly for this reason, there has not been such a great differential between unskilled and skilled wages as might be found in states to the south. Some of the cities studied had never had segregated schools and have moved slightly in that direction in spite of the new law; others have moved decisively toward integration. Some have always had peaceful relations between the two racial groups; others have some history of tension in the past. Some have been hesitant in the face of change. Others have found ways of avoiding the issue in part, somewhat as did Indianapolis. The dramatic and well-known case of Gary will be discussed separately in this book, on the grounds of its unique history and the fact that it started the process of integration before the passage of the state legislation.

Elkhart: In this city of about 36,000 people, community sentiment is more easily identified, by source and in intensity, than in larger metropolitan areas. Changes in administrative policy can be explained on a more personal level to people who are at least known to one another. By the same token, personal agreements loom large: desirable changes may be blocked by established patterns or, on the contrary, changes may be accepted even when they run somewhat counter to the local mores of the general population if their sponsor is an official whom the community respects. In Elkhart is found the story of the education of a community where appeal to reason and the democratic process removed the segregated school policy.

Not until after World War I were Negroes numerous in Elkhart; even by 1950 they represented only about 4 per cent of the total population. Most have always lived in a segregated area near and paralleling the railroad tracks, and many are employed by the New York Central railroad shops. Because of the proximity of one elementary school to this area, the Negro children attended it in the past; and while the policy was not so stated, the effect was to limit them to this one school. Until 1930 this was an unsegregated elementary school. The Elkhart high school has never been segregated.

By 1929 so many Negroes had entered this one elementary school that the Board of Education appointed a Negro teacher, the first in the system. At the time she was assigned to teach about fifteen of the fourth and fifth grade pupils who were so retarded that it was thought better to separate them from the other children. In the middle of the same year another Negro teacher was employed, and it became obvious that the board was preparing for segregation as soon as a new elementary school was completed. Until this time, the school had been bi-racial. The first Negro teacher had been told that members of the Negro community knew of the change toward segregation and that they had accepted and even welcomed it. She found, however, that the parents were far from ready when the time came, and it became her task to explain the necessity for segregation because she became the principal of the segregated school. She was unable to make this explanation satisfactorily, and her attempt to do so was resented by the Negro parents.

When the new school opened, the white children from the old school were transferred to it, leaving in the original school ninety-five Negro children and three Negro teachers. The first teacher who had been employed was given the title of principal, even though she was subordinate to, and supervised by, the white principal of the new school.

That the Negro community was opposed to the segregated policy is shown by the fact that they began a series of protests, starting before the opening of the segregated school in September, 1930, and lasting until re-integration was achieved some eighteen years later. During most of this long period, the issues centered on the rejection of a new elementary school building for the Negro children. The Elkhart Industrial Union Council, CIO, sent a resolution to the board in support of all-out opposition to any effort, or the effect of any such effort, tending toward the segregation of the Negro students. In 1947 a delegation, composed of interested Negroes and representatives of the local CIO, appeared before the board to request that the school for Negroes be closed and the children allowed to attend the school nearest their homes. After the delegation left, the minutes of the board noted, "The Board agreed that the schools as now organized serve the best purposes and interests of the pupils and the community as a whole."

The attitude of the school board at this time was expressed in a list of "Arguments Favorable to a Separate School for Negroes in Elkhart" which was prepared by the superintendent. That these were primarily the expression of diffuse, unarticulated objections to integration can be seen by their internal inconsistencies:

1. If Negroes attend a white school, only a few will be enrolled in any single classroom. They have no opportunity to compete in various activities and develop personality. They usually lose their identity and opportunity to develop.

2. On the other hand, if Negroes are permitted to attend schools reserved for Negroes, they have the opportunity to participate widely, engage in activities of their own interests and capacities, expand their own skills and accomplishments, such as vocal music, athletics, etc., and to be taught by members of their own race.

3. It should be kept in mind that Negro pupils are not required to attend the South Side School. If they insist, they may attend the white school in the district in which they live.

4. A comparison of the mental abilities of the Negro child with the white child attending the Elkhart schools shows that the Negro mental level is lower than that of the white child. This factor alone makes it wholly desirable that they be placed in separate schools. Teachers will be able to make better progress with them since they represent the homogeneous group.

5. They now have separate churches, a separate social center, and are now in the act of organizing a separate Legion Post.

6. The South Side School now has Negro teachers and a Negro custodian which they would not have if placed in the other schools.

7. The Board inherited a separate school for Negroes. If the school is disbanded and the children sent to other schools, there

is a great likelihood that parents of white children will object, which will create a problem.

8. Negro teachers are now on tenure who would have to be assigned to the white schools.

By June, 1948, the NAACP had entered the struggle; a special counsel was brought to Elkhart by the "South Siders." Her appearance before the school board was fully and favorably reported in the press. She said she thought that the city of Elkhart did not want to go to court to fight for segregation, but it might have to if it continued its present policy. At a public meeting, attended by about 100 people, both Negro and white, she said, "I can only ask you as reasonable and thinking people, to decide if it is worthwhile to you as American citizens to spend that much effort and that much money to impress on fewer than 100 Negro children that you do not like them because some of their ancestors were slaves. I hope Elkhart will solve the problem out of moral conviction, but the national offices of the NAACP are prepared to go to court if the School Board is unable to find a solution."

That her appeal was effective was shown by the meeting of more than 200 residents of the Hawthorne district, the white school district nearest the segregated one, with the school board in July, at which time they presented a three point program: 1) the immediate abandonment of the South Side School; 2) the absorption of its teachers into the school system "as roving specialists"; 3) equal distribution of the Negro pupils among the grade schools of the city, which would avoid overcrowding any one school. This is one of the few instances found in these communities in which a public meeting *before* a board decision seemed to be effective in bringing about parental acceptance of desegregation.

A week later the board announced that the South Side School would be closed, the pupils assigned to schools having room for them, and the teachers assigned wherever a vacancy existed.

Among the articulate members of the community the decision was received with enthusiasm. The files of the board contain numerous letters congratulating it. The PTA welcomed the Negro teachers into any city school, and the fears of the board that white parents would object were not borne out.

The Negro pupils were distributed among seven of the eight elementary schools. Reassignments since 1948 have increased the number in the three schools nearest the Negro district; the announced reason is that a railroad underpass, planned for the near future, will put these schools within walking distance for the children, thereby dispensing with the need for bus transportation.

The South Side School, remodeled and reopened in 1952, now has a bi-racial student body. In order to reassure the Negroes that it would not again be used as a segregated school and to dispel white parental fears, a series of fourteen forum meetings was held before the school was ready to be opened. The meetings drew about 115 people and were open to free discussion of opposition to or approval of the use of the former school for Negroes as a new integrated kindergarten-primary unit. The result was the acceptance of this school by both racial groups.

The most striking effect of the integration program, in addition to the immediate and complete way in which it was carried out, was the acceptance of the Negro teachers in schools which were predominantly white. The principal of the former segregated school was given a roving assignment to teach art in each of the schools in turn. The other two teachers were assigned to grades in different schools. There is evidence that they were liked and that there was no difficulty with the students, the large majority of whom were white. Three PTA's requested that these teachers be rotated so that all schools could have them on their faculties or, if this could not be done, that additional Negro teachers be hired.

Elkhart illustrates how sometimes an outsider, in this instance the NAACP representative, can act as a catalyst in a social situation. By bringing together the proponents and the opponents of desegregation, each group was placed in the position of defending its points logically and responsibly. In this instance the logic of desegregation won, and it won so completely that white groups then took the initiative in assuring the school board of their cooperation in the proposed program. Other communities, notably Cairo, have not been so fortunate in having impartial individuals support school desegregation as a process leading to integration.

New Albany and Jeffersonville: These two cities will be discussed together because, in contrast to Elkhart, neither of them have fully integrated faculties. Both have had somewhat more uneasy adjustments within the schools.

The Negro population of New Albany was about 4 per cent of the total population of 29,346 in 1950. Negroes are concentrated in one major and several minor areas of the city. The accommodation patterns are typically those of segregation. Negroes are excluded from restaurants, hotels, and other public places; the one exception is the theaters which were opened to them recently.

Unlike Elkhart, the School Board of New Albany was ready for the desegregation of students, primarily because of the expense of maintaining the dual system and because of the deteriorated condition of the high school for Negroes. In a paradoxical but not unusual manner, therefore, the new Indiana law pointing toward integration helped the board out of a difficult practical problem. There were a few scattered protests from parents, but the board announced its schedule for progressive integration, starting with the first grade and moving through the twelfth. Actually, as will be shown, the elementary schools still remained overwhelmingly segregated. The program at the elementary level was complete in 1950, the senior high school in 1951, and the junior high school in 1952. In 1952 there were fifty Negro students in the high school and eighteen in the desegregated elementary schools.

The children in the Griffin School were there by parental choice, at least nominally, since they were given officially the opportunity to choose another school. The answer to this seemed to be that the Negro people of New Albany were inclined to keep the school because it provided a community center in an otherwise segregated situation. Even the high school students made use of it, reportedly because informal pressures limited their participation in the extra-curricular activities in the integrated school. Griffin School also gave employment to the Negro teachers who had not been integrated into the remainder of the community's educational system.

It is reported that many Negroes felt very strongly on this point. Their position was that without integration at the faculty level, there was only toleration under the new law. At the time of the changed policy announcement, Negro teachers without tenure were dismissed; those who were retained stayed at Griffin, the Negro school. This meant that some Negro teachers were working at different levels and in different subjects than those for which they had trained. It also meant that teaching as a professional occupation was much more limited for them. Only by retaining one such school did they have any openings in this field at all.

In this city the Negro community had strong leaders who helped in the adjustments of the Negro students in the desegregated schools. The children were cautioned by their parents to go out of the way to avoid any appearance of trouble and to be cooperative within the school situation.

The student relationships seemed to be good in school. There was no trouble over Negro and white students sitting side by side or sharing lockers. Friendships appeared to have developed across racial lines, but there was no evidence that this carried over into the non-school situation. That the attitudes of parents did not change so readily appears in the composition of the PTA. The Negro parents were officially welcomed, but few availed themselves of the opportunity to attend. Some of them said that they did not feel welcome in spite of the official greeting given them.

Before integration there were seventy-five Negro students in the high school; in 1953 there were fifty. Community observers mentioned that this decrease occurred because Negro youth were not given the same encouragement to go on in school as they had been given formerly. Consistent with this portrait was the common opinion that many Negro students dropped out of school because of the less appealing social life in a desegregated school or because of the daily reminders that they belonged to a minority group. The larger pattern of segregation and discrimination seemed to influence the school situation, in spite of a school policy favoring desegregation.

Another community in transition, Jeffersonville, has a higher proportion of Negroes than New Albany. Here Negroes represented about 13 per cent of the 14,685 people in 1950. About 10 per cent of the public school student body was Negro. Desegregation has taken place at all levels, starting with the elementary schools. In the spring of 1954 there were over 50 Negroes in the high school, about 150 in the junior high school, and about 265 in the elementary schools. However, only one elementary school had an equal proportion of Negro and white children.

For a number of years, it is reported, in anticipation of integration, Negro teachers were kept from receiving tenure and were not given contracts until the new term of school opened. With the desegregation process, Negro teachers without tenure were dismissed, and those with tenure, with the exception of two persons, were transferred to non-teaching assignments. These two were assigned, respectively, to classes in speech correction and to work with mentally retarded children. Each of these classes was elective, not required. The community, in spite of its Southern sentiments, accepted this arrangement though it was suggested by some local people that the board might meet the law technically by paying the teachers for "doing nothing." Because of community sentiment it is unlikely that the superintendent would consider hiring another Negro teacher.

The school board policy on faculty integration in these two communities appears to have limited effectively teaching as a career for Negroes. There is no clear evidence that this has influenced the adjustment of Negro pupils in the elementary schools, but the testimony as to Negro enrollment and participation in the high schools is suggestive.

Evansville: This community illustrates still another technique of desegregation. Approximately 7 per cent of the 128,636 people there in 1950 were Negro. The more recent arrivals, both Negro and white, have come from the South, and many of the more established residents have customs and ideas, especially with regard to Negro-white relations, which might be expected in this location just across the river from Kentucky. In March, 1948, a year before the anti-segregation law was passed, the mayor appointed a Commission on Human Relations to work with him to reduce discrimination against Negroes. In the first year of this commission's existence, discrimination in the city parks was eliminated, a course of instruction in race relations was given to forty-two police officers, Negro police officers were given patrol cars for the first time, and more adequate hospital facilities were arranged for Negroes. Since then, segregation has been eliminated in the theaters, and in 1953 a campaign was conducted by the commission to open the restaurants for the use of all persons.

To prepare the community for integrated schools, a series of forum meetings were held in several schools to which Negro leaders were invited. The purpose was to give the school board an opportunity to assess the climate of opinion among a select group of individuals. There was some considerable pressure put on the board at these meetings to ignore the new Indiana law. However, the PTA's tended to stress the idea that the schools should take a democratic and law-abiding stand. When the board announced its policy it was able to say that its stand had been arrived at on the basis of these meetings.

The plan of the Board of School Trustees, announced in March, 1949, was definite, and the school authorities were firm in adhering to its provisions:

... in reality every child in Evansville lives in two school districts. . . . The Board of School Trustees proposes that we keep our double system of school districts, and in compliance with the (law) permit every child, who in September, 1949, enrolls in kindergarten, grade 1, or grade 9 the choice of enrolling in either of the two schools in whose district he resides. It should be emphasized that in September, 1949, only those children in the three designated grades will be given this choice. In compliance with the law the choice will gradually be extended to all children in all grades ... the system proposed would provide the people of our community with a choice, and their actions in the coming years will indicate the pattern which our schools will follow in the future. In order that the choice will not be nullified by additional costs imposed on some children, the board will continue to furnish transportation on approximately the same routes which this year served Lincoln and Third Avenue Schools.

Surprisingly few Negroes availed themselves of the new choices; only eighteen Negro children were enrolled in schools formerly for whites as the program went into effect.

The policy of the Negro parents seemed to be one of "wait and see how this is going to work." However, in subsequent years, more children (fifty in 1952) took advantage of the new possibilities. In a system such as the one in operation here, the quality of first grade instruction is most important, and apparently the Negro parents have learned that it is of very high calibre in the desegregated schools. By the fall of 1953 one Negro had entered a high school formerly for whites, and his record was very good there.

The attitude of the school administration did not seem to be the decisive factor in explaining why so few Negroes availed themselves of the wider choice in schools. Several years before desegregation, and independently of it, a program of improving the facilities of the schools for Negroes was begun so that their quality is now equal to any of the other schools. The high school for Negroes is the center of Negro cultural life.

Though one of the objections to the dual system might be that so many Negro children need to be transported to school, this is not necessarily an objection as interpreted by the Negro parents. Almost half of one elementary school enrollment was transported free by the school bus. Half of these students came from the country, and their tuition and expenses were paid by the county. To many Negro parents transportation and free lunches meant the opportunity for mothers to work outside the home until the children were returned by bus, which would be later in the day since they were not within walking distance of school. Should this school bus service be discontinued, the integration picture might possibly be quite different.

If the program is continued as it now is, it is estimated that upon completion of the process as prescribed by law and the local policy, 7.5 per cent of the Negro elementary school children might be expected to be in the desegregated schools. The increase in the first three years after 1949 was less than eleven Negro students distributed among six schools. There were still sixteen schools with only white children, some of which were in districts in which no Negroes lived.

Students interviewed appeared to prefer the high school for Negroes (Lincoln) because there they had a better chance to be in extra-curricular activities since this is a small school that plays a full schedule of sports with schools having up to five times its enrollment. Only one student interviewed mentioned fear of intimidation as a reason for remaining at Lincoln.

There was another factor, also, which probably influenced parental choice of school. As in Indianapolis, the board's policy required that Negro parents take the initiative in breaking with tradition. The good adjustment of the few students who chose the integrated system was not yet sufficiently reassuring to the majority for them to risk the change. There was also some indication that the Negro teachers, unconsciously or knowingly, favored keeping Lincoln School as a source of security. Integration of faculty was not mentioned in the policy of the school board, and the events in New Albany and Jeffersonville are well known.

In this city with almost 10,000 Negroes, the Negro teachers have a high status. There are 103 positions in the Negro schools, 83 of them teaching positions. White and Negro teachers receive the same salaries, but the Negro teacher enjoys a relatively higher status in his segregated community than does the white teacher in his. The small size of the Negro high school gives the Negro teacher a better chance to earn "extra pay for extra duties" which comes with coaching, directing music and dramatics. The essentially conservative position of the Negro teachers has been recognized by the NAACP, and it has not undertaken a campaign for teacher integration. The local chapter felt it might even encounter active and vocal resistance from the teachers were such a proposal made.

CHAPTER 5

Community in Chaos:
CAIRO, ILLINOIS *

The Background

AT FIRST GLANCE THE STORY OF CAIRO MIGHT—ALMOST—BE
taken as a portrait of any number of communities farther
south. Certainly Cairo identifies itself as Southern in its attitudes, sentiments, mores. But it cannot be assumed to fit
traditional stereotypes of Southern patterns: it is a portrait
of a unique community—a city whose people and institutions
are best understood as a phase growing out of the past. One's
first impression is a picture of extremes: little economic
security, much crisis, much prejudice and submission.

It was not the purpose of any of the studies reported in this
book to inquire into anything more than the operation of the
public school system and those areas of community life which
directly impinged upon the schools. As the Cairo study
progressed, however, it became apparent that in this case
the facts of its general community life were so basic to an
understanding of its problems with desegregation that they
had to be considered in much more detail than for the other

* Based on the report of field research prepared by Bonita Valien, Fisk
University, with the assistance of Willis A. Sutton, Jr., University of Kentucky.

communities in this book. In describing the community, wherever possible the residents will speak for themselves and for their city.

Many of Cairo's white citizens seem to be insecure both economically and socially. Negroes often bear the brunt of reactions to frustration and failure on the part of these white people. Racial prejudice is deep-seated and intense. The Negro is considered inferior; his poverty, ignorance, and social disorganization are taken as evidence of his inferiority. Whites often justify these attitudes toward Negroes on the grounds that they are lacking in intelligence, lazy, and immoral. Such attitudes provide a moral basis for their behavior toward Negroes, expressed as it is in many forms of segregation and discrimination.

Partly because of their economic dependence, Negroes have, for the most part, accepted the status ascribed to them. Traditionally, Negroes in Cairo have not seriously challenged the stereotypes of Negro mentality and character. Segregation has been generally agreed to, either unconsciously as an unquestioned matter of fact or consciously as a matter of expediency. The Negro who refused to accept an inferior position as his natural heritage was branded as an "irresponsible outsider" by many people, both Negro and white.

Cairo, "Gateway to the South," has a colorful history. Several early attempts to establish a settlement on this narrow peninsula between the Ohio and the Mississippi Rivers failed. The unfavorable climatic conditions, the low swampy land, the shifting channels of the rivers discouraged the early settlers. It was not until 1817 with the beginning of steam navigation on the rivers that Cairo's future was assured. A succession of land grant companies attempted to develop the area, failed, and were followed by still more speculators. The land companies, who set the ecological pattern of the city, "made their lots 25 x 100 feet only, and their streets 50 and

60 feet wide, with few exceptions, and dispensed with alleys altogether." [1]

The city has always had a difficult time with the rivers. In spite of the constant fight to control the channels and the high waters in the spring, many Cairo citizens will insist that the city has never been flooded. This is a point which engenders a good deal of sensitivity, so "nobody talks about a flood in Cairo." Modern Cairo consists in large part of rectangular, V-roofed, unpainted frame houses. Two avenues, originally planned to provide for the surplus trade of the Ohio levee, today comprise the business district while the shops on the levee are deserted. One avenue is lined with buildings ornamented in the mercantile emporium manner of the 1880's. What otherwise might be a quiet business district is livened by the music issuing from the taverns and other establishments which furnish much of what Cairo calls "business" and "fun."

The population of Cairo grew slowly until 1930 when it showed a decrease for the first time. The population of 12,123 in 1950 represented a decrease of 16 per cent over the 1940 figures. Of this total, the Negro made up 36 per cent. The proportion of Negroes in the total has increased each decade except the last, which recorded a decrease of 2 per cent from 1940. The Cairo Association of Commerce gives figures larger than the 1950 census reported, in the belief that "there has always been an underestimation by the census enumerators."

Official information is not available as to the origin of the majority of the native-born population. Popular belief, supported by many public officials, is that at least 90 per cent have come from the South, with western Kentucky furnishing a large proportion of this total. The population, in comparison with Illinois and the United States, is an older population.

1. John M. Lansden, *A History of the City of Cairo, Illinois* (Chicago: R. R. Donnelley and Son, 1910), 167-68.

Persons sixty-five years and over account for 11.6 per cent of its total, while for the state and nation the percentages are 8.7 and 8.2 respectively.

Educationally, Cairo's people are below the state and national average. The median school years completed by the male population twenty-five years of age and over is 8.6 as compared with 9.1 and 9.0 for the state and nation. The female population of Cairo, of the same group, compares less favorably with the women of the state and nation than do the men. The median grade completed was 8.6 as against 9.5 and 9.6 for Illinois and the United States.

As has been pointed out, Cairo shows sensitivity with regard to its population growth and composition. In spite of the census figures, the belief persists that the proportion of Negroes has always been greater than the official figure which has never exceeded one-third of the total. It is significant that the white residents are inclined to overestimate the proportion, putting it at from one-half to three-fourths of the total. This belief reflects the existing pattern of relationships and tensions between the races and sometimes is asserted as a justification for the various restrictions placed on Negroes.

Informed persons say that the power structure in the white community does not conform to the prestige positions of the pioneer families. Persons who have a relatively high economic status, but who lack family tradition, may not be considered by the first families as "really belonging" though they may be accepted into the major civic, social, and fraternal organizations. Some of the politicians and the reputed gamblers are most often mentioned as falling within this group. While at no time would they be recognized as the prestige bearers, they are known as the power group in the community. A middle class, which includes the public officials, small business men, teachers and ministers, is a respected group, most often depended upon to carry out the wishes of the larger community, especially those that relate to the sub-community of Negroes. It is through people in this group that the machinery of government operates. It appears that they gain their respect by virtue of occupation and community participation rather than wealth or family tradition.

Poverty among a large percentage of the people, and the social disorganization which often accompanies it, keeps the majority of the residents in the lowest class according to local estimates. Here are the unskilled, the occasional workers, the chronic relief group, and those who live "more by their wits than by their skills."

In the Negro community a sharp distinction is drawn between those few individuals whom the white residents consider the Negro leaders and the one Negro man whom the Negroes themselves fully respect as a leader. The Negro upper class is very small and apparently somewhat dissociated from the problems confronting the bulk of the Negro residents.

The Negro middle class is made up of such professional persons as the doctors, teachers, and principals, and the more important business men of the area. This is the group to be depended on to maintain the *status quo* according to Cairo residents. Some variations must be noted, however. The teachers and principals, dependent on the white school board, sometimes serve as the interpreters for the dominant group and have been assisted in this task by the Negro ministers. These are the professions whose members feared loss of position or prestige when desegregation was started. Greater economic independence of other middle-class families makes them less amenable to the white community. It is reported that historically Negro doctors could be depended on to cooperate with the white community; within recent years, however, some of them have become strong opponents of the accepted pattern of racial subordination. Representing a younger and more mobile group, the more recent professional persons have been referred to as "outsiders," "radicals," "agitators," and "reds" by the white people.

As in the white population, the majority of Negroes are found in the lowest socioeconomic level, but unlike the whites they appear to be less homogeneous. A disproportionate number of Negroes are concentrated at this level. Both Negro and white informants said that these people preferred dealing with the white members of the police, the relief agency, and other official bodies, because they did not want other Negroes to know the true state of their affairs. Nevertheless, here are found the people who, recognizing their own limitations, seek better opportunities for their children. It was in this group that parents encouraged their children to go to the desegregated schools when an opportunity presented itself. A conspicuous failure of the upper and middle classes to enter their children in these schools has been pointed to as one of the contributing factors to the tension among many Negroes at the time of the school struggle.

There is a common saying locally that "politics is buying nigger votes." Cairo people generally say that the Negro vote is controlled, and it is necessary to the election of any official. Some Negroes feel strongly about this. One said:

Now I've been in Cairo all my life, and I know this thing, how it works. It's a shame how these people, both poor whites and Negroes act on election day. Of course . . . the politician comes around near election time, gives these niggers some whiskey and a sandwich, and tells them, "Now you will go and vote for so and so there's more coming where that come from." And you know these people go and throw away their vote for a drink and a sandwich . . . one of my neighbors said, "I always makes them pay me. . . . I don't never vote unless they pays me in front." Can you beat that?

Lack of knowledge, lack of confidence in the ability of the Negro leadership to exercise authority if elected, and extreme poverty are important factors influencing the behavior of

Negroes who allow themselves to be used in what most residents call "Cairo's dirty politics."

Negroes have long figured prominently in the law enforcement agencies in the city. In 1953 of the eleven regular patrolmen, three were Negro; and six of the twenty-three auxilliary patrolmen were Negro. In the county there were Negroes who served as justices of the peace, constables, sheriff, and deputy coroner. However, general opinion is that these officers are expected to handle Negro cases or, at best, to "assist" should an incident involve a white person.

The reputed success of the Negro police with the Negro offenders may have something to do with the acceptance of the myth that it takes a Negro to handle a Negro. As stooges, so called by many Negroes, the Negro police are thought to carry information between the two communities. During the school desegregation process, Negro policemen, along with some of the Negro ministers and teachers, fulfilled the function of locating and advising families who were on public assistance that if they sent their children to the desegregated schools, they would be removed from relief rolls.

Police records do not reveal that Negroes are arrested any more or less frequently than are whites. However, some white informants believed that Negroes were arrested less frequently and referred to the police as "nigger lovers."

By any standard used to judge the adequacy of housing, Cairo vies with one other Illinois city for the lowest rating in the state. Of all urban centers of 10,000 or more population, Cairo had the lowest per cent of dwelling units with electric lights (93), the lowest with radio (88) and, together with Harrisburg, the lowest with kitchen sinks (75). In addition, together with West Frankfort, Cairo had the lowest proportion of dwelling units with hot running water, private toilets, and baths in units not considered delapidated (49).

To these conditions is added the locally recognized prevalence of overcrowding and difficult sanitation problems. Garbage cans on the front walks, because there are no alleys, numerous areas of the city filled with cans and other debris to eliminate low places, rows of outdoor privies without sewage connection and without regular inspection for cleanliness all help to give most parts of the city what some local people called "the appearance of a slum."

While there are more Negroes in some precincts than in others, Negroes live scattered throughout fifteen of the sixteen precincts. Thus, residential segregation is not so sharp as in many Southern and some Northern cities. Negroes occupy about 37 per cent of all dwelling units in the city, but only about 22 per cent of the owner-occupied ones. More than 77 per cent of the Negro houses were rented, and the rented dwelling units usually were more dilapidated than the owner-occupied ones.

Contributing to the perpetuation of this situation is the absence of municipal regulations or public programs regarding housing and absentee ownership of rental property. Together with the low economic level of the people who occupy the rented houses, white people generally believe that Negroes from the South are responsible for the appearance of the homes of the city.

With reference to the lack of regulations or concern on the part of the city, one influential white resident said:

There has never been a concerted effort on the part of the city officials to do anything about housing. The attitude of the first land owners—to get all they could with the least expenditure still characterizes municipal thinking with reference to housing. The land owners look upon property primarily as a source of income. ... The average land owner ... will rent a place until it collapses, draining it of everything it has, before he will spend a penny on the upkeep. Both ignorance and greed are responsible. Cairo is a greedy city, that's why it's such a miserable town in its social values. ...

As to absentee ownership, one Negro renter whose walls were stuffed with paper and rags for protection from the weather said of her landlord:

The woman who owns this house lives in Chicago now; she has one of her friends collect the rent. When I point out certain things that need to be done, her friend says she will tell her, and that's the last I hear. . . . I pay $20 a month for this place . . . it isn't worth that. . . . I stay because it is a pretty good neighborhood, near my friends and the church. Then, if I leave it just means going to the same or worse. At least the foundations of this house is high enough not to be pestered with seep water. I have a lot of friends who have to move out of their houses at some times because the water gets so high it comes right on up through the floor. . . .

In defense, a landlord explained his position:

There's not much upkeep you can do out of the low rent we get for these places. As little as the rent is, these people aren't able to pay that. Further, when they have a decent home to live in they won't keep it up. . . . We have our problems, too, you see.

Though admitting that the housing situation in Cairo leaves much to be desired, and although dilapidated structures are by no means limited to the Negroes, the white citizens believed that much of Cairo's housing problem is tied up with "the way of life of the colored people who have come from rural areas into Cairo."

Associated with this type of housing is the predominance of outdoor privies, the majority of which have no sewage connection, and the city assumes no responsibility either for their cleaning or inspection. This condition not only represents the source of a health menace, but through lack of cleaning it is highly offensive.

Such is Cairo's housing. The difficulties find their varying interpretations in the different segments of the population. Each interpretation, bolstered by what appeared to be a lack of municipal concern, produces fatalistic attitudes toward the possibility of changing the present patterns of living.

Cairo's present economy is considered precarious. The median income for families and unrelated persons in 1950 was $1,553 as compared with $3,163 for the state and $2,619 for the nation. In Cairo almost 59 per cent of the population had a yearly income of less than $2,000. Public officials supported the prevailing opinion that in 1953 Cairo was heavily dependent on the operation of the two atomic energy plants near by. Until they opened, the city was "just about dead," said one business man. Faith in Cairo's future was not one of the strong points made by local citizens.

A study of the active files in the office of the Illinois State Employment Service at the end of June, 1953, revealed that 41 per cent of the total applicants from the Cairo area were less than thirty-five years old, while only 4 per cent were more than sixty-five. About two-thirds of all applicants were unskilled workers or agricultural harvest hands; the remainder were in the various other classifications. The statement was made that Cairo is usually an area where a considerable surplus exists in the labor market. Seasonal factors in the agricultural region surrounding the city contribute to the decline in employment in the late spring months. The bulk of the seasonal workers are Negroes.

Negroes constitute less than 2 per cent of the skilled workers in Cairo. Besides the Negro professionals and business men there were only two Negroes, who could be located during the period of the survey, who were actually employed and receiving pay as skilled workers. This excludes workers at the near-by atomic energy plants. Officials of the employment service felt that there was nothing to indicate that employment opportunities would increase in the near future. They reported that jobs for Negro high school graduates were so hard to find that their office had been placing such youth with the veterans hospital nearby as attendants and kitchen help.

There is but one hospital in Cairo, and the policy is to segregate Negro and white patients. Until recently there was but one ward for Negroes, and both sexes had to be accommodated there. For a time Negro women were not allowed to use the delivery room, and their babies were born in this ward. Recently the accommodations have been somewhat improved, by partitioning the ward and turning a utility room into semi-private rooms for Negroes. Until about a decade ago, Negro doctors were allowed to practice in the hospital; since then they have not been granted this privilege, nor does there seem any likelihood that a change will take place in the near future.

For many years a large percentage of Cairo's population has been in need of some type of public assistance. "As long as I can remember, we have had large relief rolls," stated a public official. "We get most of our people from the South, they get stranded here, and we have to take care of them . . . until such time as they get able to take care of themselves. It's a curious thing, those who get able, leave Cairo; those who seem to lack initiative remain."

The reason given most frequently for the large number of persons receiving relief in recent years is the fact that Illinois' law is more liberal than those of the neighboring states. In the county as a whole, about one-tenth of the people receive relief of some kind, exclusive of emergency assistance.

The influence of politics in the area of public welfare was not a subject of the present study. However it was repeatedly described locally as following some such pattern as this:

The "big bosses" work through the precinct committeemen who locate all the people on public assistance rolls. They tell them that if they vote for a certain candidate, this allotment will be increased. They move from this group to people who are not receiving aid, promising them that they will be put on the rolls if they support a particular candidate. Few people understand the difference between the benefits as a part of the larger Social Security program and the state program of emergency assistance. After an election the public assistance office is flooded with people who expect to receive relief for the vote they cast. The officials sometimes have difficulty in convincing applicants that this is not the criterion on which relief is granted.

Some citizens said that during the school desegregation disturbance the threat of removal from relief rolls was the most persistent method used to discourage parents from sending their children to the desegregated schools. Even the director of Public Aid was approached by white persons who demanded that some Negroes be removed. The Department of Public Welfare estimated that over half the total relief roll was Negro, with Aid to Dependent Children grants representing the largest group.

Most public and non-governmental facilities in Cairo are segregated. There are thirty-seven churches, sixteen of which are Negro. There are thirty-seven taverns, most of which are segregated, though in some it is possible for Negroes to be served if they stand at the bar. The three movies are segregated (one is a Negro theater); the drive-in accommodates both races. There is a municipal park, divided down the middle by a walk "so the races won't mix," and a swimming pool, built with WPA funds, "Sponsored and Operated by the Cairo Rotary Club," for whites only. It is possible for Negroes to take books out of the municipal library, but they are not given library cards, a point of some sensitivity to both groups. There is a scantily equipped branch of the library in the Negro high school, and it is to this that the Negroes turn. Considering the general level of education and interest, of course, neither library is currently of much interest to the majority of Cairo's citizens. There is no restaurant operated by whites which will serve food to Negroes at tables or, in drug stores, at the counter. One white restaurant owner, commenting on his refusal to serve NAACP officials during the school desegregation disturbance, gave a standard explanation:

It wasn't that I didn't want to serve them, but I've got my life savings here, and if I let them come in, I wouldn't have anything else. It would ruin me. I just couldn't serve them. I'll cash in first because I might as well if it comes to that.

After the desegregation program started, signs appeared in some public eating houses stating, "This establishment reserves the right to select its clientele."

Because Cairo has been described as a "sick city," not only by outsiders but by some residents themselves, it has seemed pertinent to consider in detail some of the factors which may have influenced the attitudes of its citizens and the procedures used by officials during the initial consideration of desegregation. The preceding description indicates that many factors other than the administration of the schools converged to make of this problem an issue almost impossible of amicable settlement.

Desegregation in Process

With such a portrait of a community it seems evident that some outside strength would be needed to bring about even a slight change in local mores. Outside forces came to bear on the situation from two sources: the greater effectiveness of the Illinois school laws, which were amended in 1949 and again in 1951 in an effort to assure desegregation of schools in the southern part of the state; and in increased activities of the NAACP in Cairo.

From the time the first anti-segregation law was passed in Illinois in 1874, there were numerous additions and amendments designed to maintain a desegregated system within the state. However, the southern counties continued to ignore the provisions, and in 1949 the General Assembly provided in the school desegregation bill (House Bill 1066) that state funds would be withheld from counties with segregated schools. At the sessions in 1951, an amendment was passed which stated:

No state aid claim may be filed for any district unless the clerk or secretary of the school board executes and files with the Superintendent of Public Instruction . . . a sworn statement that the district has complied with the requirements of Section 6-37 in regard to non-segregation of pupils on account of race, color, or nationality.[2]

At the same time the House passed a resolution (No. 34) which set up a legislative committee to investigate compliance with Section 4 of House Bill 1066 cited above.

The special committee appointed by the House of Representatives of the Illinois State Assembly subpoenaed thirteen county superintendents of schools to investigate what action they had taken to comply with the Jenkins Amendment to the Distributive Fund Appropriations Bill. At the hearings the county superintendent of schools of Alexander County said that it was not her fault that the schools were segregated and that she would be more than willing to aid in ending segregation. She did, in fact, hold up state aid funds in the spring and for a short time in the fall of 1951.

In its written report, the special committee noted that in Alexander County neither the county superintendent of schools, nor the district superintendent, nor the school trustee board "are doing anything about obeying the law." The committee called the attention of the attorney general and the superintendent of public instruction to this. Specifically in Alexander County, the committee concluded that the superintendent of the Cairo schools was "the main obstacle to the elimination of segregation" and called attention to a state-

2. Illinois Laws, House Bill 1066.

ment made under oath by the acting secretary of the Cairo Board of Education stating that the schools were in compliance with the law.

At the time of the investigation, the superintendent stated that no Negroes had requested transfers to schools for whites, and it was on this ground that he secured release of the state aid funds. No public statement had been made regarding desegregation, and since there were no school districts or zones for school purposes in Cairo, nor any militant leadership among the Negroes, there the matter rested for a time.

The first public school established for Negroes in Cairo had opened in 1872, and the dual system has been in effect ever since. In 1950, there were eleven public schools: seven elementary, three of which were for Negroes; two junior high, one for each race; and two senior high schools, one for each. The dual system, as it was organized, has best been described as a dominant system and a wardship, with the schools for Negroes under the control and direction of the white school administration. The two sets of schools operated completely as separate units; there was no contact between white and Negro teachers except that which was offered at the beginning and end of the year when the superintendent addressed them, with the Negroes seated on one side of the room and the whites on the other. From this point on, the Negro principal was the only point of contact between the Negro teachers and the white school administration. His actions were criticized by some Negroes; one person put it this way, "He is expected to keep the Negro teacher satisfied with an inferior status in the system."

There was alleged to be another contact, but it existed only on paper. In order to avoid the equal salaries required by law, it is reported, some white teachers were listed as department heads of the schools for Negroes though they had no personal contact with the school. There were no Negro department heads. Because of this limited contact, the

Negro teacher had little or no knowledge of what was provided in the school for whites. One teacher commenting on this said, "What's in the white school? That's like death, nobody's been through it to tell about it."

Thus the schools for Negroes in Cairo were said to have responsibility without authority. Their serious lack of equipment and limited curriculum offerings, added to the generally low standards of performance, made them less than equal to the schools for whites in the same city.

The external appearance, with few exceptions, of the schools for whites and Negroes was not much different, because both seemed sub-standard in comparison with other communities. The Special Committee of the Assembly noted that the high school for Negroes was inadequate and overcrowded, with little or no library facilities. One of the elementary schools for Negroes had old fashioned privies, a small playground, and the building was old, miserably equipped, with poor lighting, and no plumbing except face bowls. In spite of this report the school superintendent insisted that the two school systems were equal in every respect, the curriculum offerings the same, and where differences appeared in the physical structure, it was a matter of upkeep rather than one of a basically inferior structure.

It was after the superintendent's skirmish with the state authority that the local branch of the NAACP invited the national office to give assistance in a membership drive, with desegregation of schools as the main interest. Early in January, 1952, two representatives of the national association were assigned to work in Cairo. Each had a good record of conciliation in other communities facing similar problems. When they met with the local branch, plans were made for a mass meeting on January 6, and the radio carried spot announcements to this effect throughout the days of the fifth and the sixth.

The meeting was attended by approximately 500 people.

The NAACP representatives explained the work of the organization and discussed the state law in regard to desegregated schools. Negro parents were encouraged to try to register their children in the schools for whites at the beginning of the next semester which was to open on January 28.

On January 11, the NAACP conducted a fifteen-minute radio forum, on which the local president and the two national representatives cited the state law within the framework of national problems facing minority groups.

On January 15 they attended a conference with the school authorities and requested information on a number of points:

1. What was the program of the school officials going to be when faced with requests for transfer from Negro schools?

2. Would the school officials publicly state their position?

3. Granting such transfers were made, what procedures were to be followed?

4. What plans had been made by the school board for preparing school personnel for the change, and what program would be undertaken?

5. Would the school board welcome the assistance of a representative group of citizens in working out problems which might arise?

6. What would be the program of the school officials with regard to the integration of Negro teachers as well as students?

The school board indicated that it would accept any child in any school, qualifying the statement to indicate that the transfer would have to be initiated by the child's parents. There was some indication that up to this point the board had not thought that any Negro children would ask for transfers.

The board did not think that any public statement was necessary. A pattern of procedures was worked out, the school officials stipulating that they preferred requests to come from parents at the beginning of a semester. It was understood that twenty-four hours would be necessary to process transfers through the pupil's teacher, the principals involved, and the superintendent's office. The board felt that no advance preparation of school personnel was needed. No plans were being considered for reassigning teachers since, the officials stated, they were hired on the basis of qualifications, not on race. It was the opinion of the group attending the meeting that the school board seemed to feel that a citizens' committee was not desired; the board was non-committal as to cooperation should such a committee be established. The board said that it would consider these matters further but indicated that the NAACP group would not be welcomed at any further meetings.

One of the school officials interpreted the meeting as one in which he met with "a group of outsiders who were absolutely unreasonable; they didn't care for the individual, it was all for the race. They wanted us to district the whole town; we refused and we'll never do that."

The increase in tension in the community dated from this meeting. For the first time, apparently, the school authorities realized that they were no longer going to be able to avoid some gesture in the direction of desegregation, no matter how distasteful to them or to others in the community. This situation provides an excellent example of a community in which there were no impartial persons able to mediate differences between heated opponents. Having earlier ignored the possibility of desegregation, no one was neutral in the ensuing conflict.

Following the meeting the NAACP circulated mimeographed sheets among the Negro community; one was "Know Your Rights in Public Schools"; the other, "Explanation for Monday's Procedure." The latter outlined the transfer procedure to be followed on the opening day of the new semester, Monday, January 28. According to NAACP figures, there were about eighty-four requests for transfers at this time.

In the two weeks between the meeting with the school

board and the opening of the new semester, the vested interests of the two groups, and of individuals within each group, became increasingly apparent. There were resistances and veiled and open threats of retaliation among the white residents; within the Negro upper and upper middle class, not one family had asked for the transfer of its children. This hesitancy to disturb the prevailing pattern apparently stemmed in part from the fear of retaliation in business or professional ways by the white citizens of Cairo. The one professional man who was active in the fight for desegregation indicated that he would have sent his children to the school for whites but for the fact that they were not yet of school age. The doctors claimed some white patients, the business men had some white customers, the school staffs were obviously under the control of the white school board, the ministers depended on the bounty of the white community to some extent. Parents requesting transfers were for the most part people who had very little to lose and much to gain through the better education they were convinced their children would receive. Some claimed that they were threatened with removal from relief; and some reconsidered and withdrew applications. Other parents decided to carry through requests for transfers, on the grounds that "it had to come sometime, and this seemed as good a time as any."

From the time of the meeting with the school board, there seems to have been no further direct contact between those interested in promoting desegregation and the white officials whose responsibility it was to formulate the procedure to be followed. Channels of communication were completely closed, the radio and the newspaper refused further cooperation, and the NAACP, as well as the white board, had to work in a vacuum. The contacts with the Negro community were also less personal, more circumscribed. Each group withdrew from all others, and the resulting tensions were noticeable throughout the whole community.

That the white community was intense in its opposition to the integration program was obvious although it was thought that only the "hoodlum element" had anything to do with the extra-legal means used to intimidate those who were working for desegregation. On January 23 the white NAACP lawyer reported that his home had been stoned and that he had received several threats. Anonymous letters and telephone calls were received by the Negroes active in the program. White business men and professional men refused to serve the family of the white lawyer who represented the NAACP.

Not only was there opposition from the white residents. Among the Negroes the groups most active in attempts to discourage transfer were the ministers, Negro policemen, Negro teachers, and principals. Each had a vested interest in maintaining the *status quo*. Some Negroes said that the police told them "what the white people were not going to stand for." They said that those who persisted in attempting to enter children in the schools for whites against the wishes of the whites would be taken off the relief rolls. There is some suggestion that this did happen in a few cases.

Similarly the ministers, with one exception, "put aside their heavenly mission and devoted their full time as advisers against desegregation." One minister was said to have taken this assignment so seriously that he visited every family who had indicated interest in the change to remind them that they were very dependent on the white man in time of need, and that the NAACP was an outside group, not interested in the welfare of the local people. Apparently he induced some families who had requested transfers to withdrew their requests.

The Negro school personnel were most bitter in their attacks on those wanting desegregation. The arguments they used in talking against it varied from lack of employment if children insisted on going to schools for whites, through lack

of understanding by white teachers of Negro children's problems, to direct verbal attacks on the NAACP, its leaders, and
local supporters. The principals emphasized in talking to the
youths involved that they would not be allowed to participate
in extra-curricular activities, that the white teachers and
students would mistreat them, and that it was a reflection
on their own race to want to go to the desegregated school.
Tension and suspicion mounted throughout the Negro community.

Recognizing the imminent possibility of riots, the various
representatives of the law enforcement agencies made detailed plans intended to insure that no major race disturbances occurred. The director of the Illinois Commission on
Human Relations said, "In my limited experience I have
never seen as complete preparation on the part of the law
enforcement agencies in advance of a racial disorder. The
local police force had been tripled in size through the use of
their auxiliary police; the sheriff's force was present and the
sheriff had asked for and received the cooperation of the
State Police; the FBI was likewise alerted in case of a violation of a Federal statute."

The night before the new term was to start, crosses were
burned in the areas of highest concentration of transfer requests. Despite the cross burnings, the tension, and fears,
some Negro parents took their children to the schools for
whites the following morning. A group of white citizens
which had formed near one of the schools was dispersed by
the police, and no further groups allowed to form.

On the Friday before the term opened, the superintendent
had announced in the schools for Negroes that those children
requesting transfers should appear at their old schools and
await further instructions there. The Negroes, interpreting
this as a delaying tactic, did not follow the order. When they
reported for the new term to schools for whites, they were
told to go to the schools for Negroes or to go home. All but

two parents took the children home. When they appeared at the schools for whites again on the following day the same thing happened. By the end of the week, less than ten children had been transferred to the schools formerly for whites. The superintendent stated that he had intended to transfer about twenty but had been prevented from this because the children were not in school. However, from his remarks to a public official on another occasion it appeared that he had not intended to transfer them all on the first day of school, but a few at a time. This contradicted his earlier statement that the children should be transferred at the beginning of a new term.

One who was there said that as darkness fell on Cairo on the evening of January 29, "I have never seen a city so tense; everybody appeared to be armed and there was a silence that was almost frightening." This silence was broken about eleven o'clock at night when a bomb exploded on the back steps of the home of a Negro physician. Although no one was injured, the property damage was considerable, not only to this house but to the one next door in which a white family lived. Another bomb, its fuse out, was found in front of a Negro business establishment the next day. While there is no doubt that the white community was practically unanimous in its opposition to the desegregation program, such acts of violence were deplored and blamed on the "hoodlum element."

The police began investigations immediately, and within a few days had arrested three men, charging them with the bombings and the cross burnings. Guards were placed at the homes of the local NAACP leaders to prevent further violence. By this time the town was seething with varying currents and factions. The Negro community was divided in its opinion as to the advisability of pursuing the campaign to end segregation. Some transfer requests were withdrawn, but most continued in their determination to see the school system follow the state law.

On February 7, seven Negro leaders and the white attorney for the NAACP were arrested on a complaint warrant signed by two white business men. They were charged with "unlawfully, maliciously and wickedly" conspiring to place two Negro children "in such a situation that their life and health were endangered in that they did unlawfully, willfully and wickedly force the said children to attend Cairo Junior High School of the city of Cairo against their will."

The hearings and testimony on February 21 resulted in no true bills being returned against the Negro leaders and also no true bills against twenty-one persons charged with conspiracy in the bombing of the Negro doctor's house and the cross burnings. The NAACP immediately protested the decision with regard to the conspirators and requested the attorney general of the state to use the power of his office to take action in the failure of the county authorities to act properly. As a result, two additional grand juries were assembled. One rendered a no true bill, the other rendered one true bill against the man charged with the bombing. He was tried by the judge in his office, found guilty, and given a year's suspended sentence.

The Situation Since Desegregation

As a result of the threats, intimidations, and violence attending the first entrance of Negroes into the schools formerly for whites, by the end of the spring semester there were only seventeen Negro children in the desegregated schools, with a maximum of six in one school. Informants said that there was still considerable effort on the part of the school board to discourage any further transfers.

At the beginning of the fall term in 1952, a technique alleged to have been used to some extent was to register all the white children first and then say that there was no room for the Negro children without overcrowding the school. Some few Negroes were registered to keep the board within the law. This was the experience of one parent as he took his daughter to the junior high school:

The day of registration I was there bright and early. Nobody bothered me—nobody appeared to be interested one way or the other. When I saw the registration line form I got in it with my daughter. When my turn came, the principal who was registering said he couldn't register me at that point, that I would have to wait. When I asked him wait for what, he seemed nervous and lost for words. He then said something to the effect that he didn't know how many children would be registering. . . . Well, I just stood my ground calmly but firmly, indicating that I didn't see what that had to do with me. Finally after it became obvious that I intended to register my daughter the principal, after consultation with the superintendent, registered her. Before leaving the school that day I saw that she had her book list, locker key, and everything she needed. The woman who gave me the locker key seemed real surprised that my daughter had been registered, but I appeared not to notice it.

Parents who were not so firm reported that it some instances some children were as late as a month or more transferring from the schools for Negroes.

While the estimates of the white citizens showed some element of wishful thinking in placing the number of Negro children in the integrated schools at not more than twenty, at the end of the school year there were sixty students distributed among five schools, a maximum of nineteen in the junior high school and seventeen in one grade school.

There was no advance preparation either of the faculty or the white student body before the Negro children appeared. The attitude of the administration was that it should not be discussed and should be handled as quietly as possible. It was reported that the faculty inferred that they were not to go out of their way to be nice to the Negro children, but they were to avoid any incidents.

This alertness to possible tension resulted in one amusing experience. A girl brought a collection of rocks to school to exhibit in her geology class. They were heavy, and she left them on the school steps momentarily. The teachers saw them, assumed that they had been gathered by white students to attack the Negroes, and took them into custody. The girl had a hard time for a few minutes locating her exhibits.

Actually, within the school situation itself there was very little evidence of tension or acts of intolerance among the children. White teachers and administrators said, however, that the children who transferred represented for the most part the "worst element among the Negro population." Some teachers thought that the Negro students with whom they had any contact were sub-normal and very backward in their studies.

In general, the teachers at the elementary schools described the attitudes of white children toward Negro children as friendly, with a less favorable attitude in the upper grades. High school teachers interpreted the attitude of white students as more or less neutral, not necessarily hostile. "At first Negroes were an oddity; now they are ignored," declared one principal.

The white teacher reflected community attitudes—the Negro is all right as long as he stays in his place, and Negroes are better off in their own schools. However, both the teachers and the administrators apparently tried to be objective in their dealings with the Negro students. One principal reported that, in the beginning, he had some minor disciplinary problems with some of his white students. He told them that this was just making matters worse for everyone since the school was only obeying the law. He felt that both white students and teachers had to make the best of it, whether or not they liked it. While the greatest pressure against the program came from the upper-class white parents, once the program was approved the "incidents" in the schools were the result, not of the children from these homes, but from the lower socioeconomic class. These incidents were minor, occurred in the first few weeks of the program and only in the higher grades in school.

White teachers felt, and Negro administrators confirmed, that many students who transferred were not the best academically. The better students had been persuaded by the arguments put up by the Negro teachers and principals to remain in the Negro schools. As one Negro teacher said, "Why should we let all our good students go?" None of the students who transferred had good enough grades to be allowed to participate in school sports.

White high school students questioned about the situation expressed these general attitudes. Most felt that the Negroes had been "stirred up by outsiders" and that "they were paid" to try to get into the white schools. This was a persistent rumor for months: the NAACP had paid each family who sent a child to the integrated schools. Like all such rumors, it could not be traced to a specific source, but it continued to be believed by many white citizens. The white students were of the opinion that most white students did not like having Negroes in their classes but that the only thing to do about it was to ignore them. However, they did not think that the students minded as much as their parents.

All the examples of tension between the two races in the schools seemed to point to the white students as the instigators of unpleasantness and to the fact that the Negro students had to be very self-contained to remain in the schools during the initial period.

White students felt that the teachers protected the Negroes and indicated that this teacher attitude did keep overt hostility at a minimum. "The white students for the most part were afraid; they knew that they would be punished if they molested the Negroes." Only in a few schools did the teachers talk to the white students and give them any suggestions about how to accept Negroes. There was no indication that the attitudes of the white youth had changed materially toward the Negro youth, except that a small group of white students, who never had been accepted in the school activities, defended the Negro students and talked to them during the recreation periods.

Negro students interviewed said without exception that both they and their parents had been put under pressure by members of the Negro community to remain in the Negro schools. Their playmates said, "I'll bet those white teachers are sure going to beat you; they don't want you in their schools and they are going to be mean to you." The younger children made the change because their parents took them to the new schools, but the junior and senior high school youth wanted to change to get the benefit of a better curriculum. They were aware of the fact that graduates from their school had to make up work after graduation before they were accepted in any college. The Negro principal and the teachers are said to have made vigorous efforts to keep the youth where they were.

Several of the children said that they had never thought it possible to go to the school with white children until the NAACP had told them "their rights" with regard to schooling and their parents "became interested" in seeing them go. All indicated that the NAACP had been the primary influence, with their parents encouraging them to follow the NAACP's recommendations. There was a tendency, though not a strong one, for the children themselves to be influenced by a friend who had decided to enter a desegregated school.

All the interviews with elementary school children indicated that they were treated well when they entered the desegregated school for the first time. They said further that they liked their teachers very much; "they were real good to us," said one child. On the other hand, high school students found their first days unpleasant. "They did everything they could to discourage us, but we knew we had a right to be there. We were determined, but don't let anyone kid you, it was plenty rough at first." Many in their answers revealed the mechanisms of defense they had built up to bolster their courage. These had to be used at home and with playmates who had not transferred, as well as in the new situation. These students were under a great strain to justify, in the eyes of the community and for their own self-esteem, their action in making the transfer.

According to the testimony of the persons interviewed, no Negro child who entered the elementary schools seemed to have had an unpleasant experience with a teacher. The experiences of the junior and senior high school youth were not so uniformly pleasant, but all said that the prejudiced teachers, or those who showed prejudice, were in the minority. They felt that discipline was impartial, and that they were not discriminated against in the matter of grades. This latter point is significant since none of the Negro students kept up a scholastic average high enough to participate in sports. The exceptions to this impression that impartiality was shown in assigning grades occurred in the first marking period and soon disappeared.

In comparing the Negro and white teachers, Negro high school students had a tendency to prefer the white teacher. While they did not feel that the white teacher was "necessarily a better teacher," either from the point of view of preparation or competence in instruction, they all agreed that white teachers were stricter, and as a result they felt that they had learned more. Commenting on this, one Negro student said,

In the white school, if you don't get your lesson the teacher will make you stay in and they stay right in with you and teach you. If you do work that is not acceptable, they make you do it over again until it is. In the colored school, if you don't get your lesson, nobody seems to bother you. You just get an "E" for not knowing. Seemingly, the white teachers are more interested in making you get your lessons than the colored teachers are.

Even at the elementary school level, Negro students recognized a difference between Negro schools and desegregated schools. Said one fifth grade student, "In the white school, you are taught English and grammar, while they don't pay too much attention to this in the Negro school. Also in the Negro school they tell you about history, you don't have a book; in the white school, you have a book and you read about history. You just seem to learn more when you have a book."

In concluding this case study, attention should be focused on some of the fundamental factors involved. In Cairo, although the historical relationships between Negro and white could not by any index be viewed as entirely harmonious, the school desegregation program heightened the feeling of resentment between the two groups. There was much more consciousness of race, more effort to look for hidden meanings, greater suspicion, and a hostility that seemed nearer the surface than in the past. In spite of efforts to keep it covered, the situation was volatile, potentially explosive, even in the beginning.

The total lack of a tradition of mutual discussion or of channels for such discussions made this difficult situation an almost impossible one. After the initial steps taken under the auspices of the NAACP, there was no across-the-board contact between the two races during the transition. The contact was circuitous, making it all but inevitable that grave distortions of fact circulated in both groups. Relations, which were strained in the beginning, worsened so rapidly that the groups became more and more defensive and antagonistic and determined to win. The community was left with a leadership vacuum. There was no voice for the total community, no impartial judge around whom people of good will could rally. Since there was no public leadership to work toward new definitions of the situation, experiences were interpreted entirely in terms of the old traditions and definitions. Prejudices were reinforced on both sides. New myths arose to satisfy new needs for rationalizations. Hardly any white citizens were aware of the fundamental motivations of the Negro in desiring to enter the white schools; there was little understanding of the problem in relation to the total patterns of segregation and discrimination.

Because there was no effort to give new orientation and explanation for the children of either group, there was no ideological basis from which white children of good will could operate with confidence of support from authorities in their efforts to adjust to the Negro children. There was a rather complete ignorance on the part of the Negro children of what to expect or how to prepare themselves for emotional shocks. The unhappiness among Negro children was not lessened by their parents' pride and the hostile attitudes of their former playmates; they were left without persons in whom they could confide or to whom they could look for guidance.

The fact that some of the least able Negro children were among the first entrants into the desegregated schools reinforced the white stereotypes of Negroes' abilities and intelligence. This also increased the difficulty of the few white persons who might have helped in the adjustments of the students.

Cairo seemed almost wholly incapable of developing indigenously any plan or program of action for meeting this problem realistically. The legalistic approach, lack of preparation of either school staffs, administrators, or students, prevented mutual good will or understanding, except on a completely individual basis.

At the same time, the lack of local resources for effecting desegregation meant that movement could occur only through stimulation from outside the city. And this extra-local influence was immediately subject to the label of "interference by outsiders." The original issues were overlaid by new hostilities and recriminations.

With all this, desegregation did occur. Turmoil died away. The community reluctantly settled into a new pattern. As this study ended, the "integration" of the Negro students in this situation was still largely that of physical occupancy of space within the schools. Modern education deals with the total personality, and true integration would entail much more than this. That some cooperation and understanding did develop was not part of any plan. The children were having a broader experience and were getting along reasonably well with white classmates in spite of the strains and tensions in the relationship. White citizens were learning that the world did not come to an end.

CHAPTER 6

Reaction to Shock:
GARY AND SOUTH BEND, INDIANA *

THESE TWO INDIANA CITIES WILL BE DISCUSSED SEPARATELY here because they share some characteristics not common to the other Indiana communities in this sample. Each met the problem of desegregation before the enactment of state legislation and at a period in its history when the Negro population was increasing rapidly. Each has moved decisively to make integrated schools a fully realized fact rather than a token gesture, and each has had the help of both school personnel and community groups in the study of human relations.

In Gary integration was hastened by school strikes during 1945-1946. With the exception of Cairo, this is the only city in the survey in which overt disturbances were related to the school situation. By contrast, South Bend presents a vivid illustration of a community which has never had segregated schools but is apparently moving in that direction in spite of a firm policy of integration. This is a result of residential segregation which limits freedom of action of the school administration.

* Based on the report of field research prepared by Harold T. Christensen and Dwight W. Culver, Purdue University; and John Gandy, Assistant Research Director of the Welfare Council of Metropolitan Chicago.

Gary

Treatment of Gary can be brief because there is available already a detailed study of the school strikes.[1] Nearly 29 per cent of Gary's population of 134,000 in 1950 were Negro; another 10 per cent were foreign born. These facts influenced the schools as much as they did the total atmosphere of the city. Gary is a relatively new town. It was built and for many years controlled as a company town by the United States Steel Corporation. In these ways it is atypical although many other United States cities also have similar problems involving the relationships between large minority groups and the native white population. The proportion of Negroes in Gary increased from 18 per cent in 1940 to 29 per cent in 1950. Many of those who made up the increase were recent migrants from rural areas of the South who work primarily as unskilled laborers in the industrial plants of the city. Because the racial composition of Gary is so different from the surrounding homogeneous rural areas of Midwestern farm folk, the distinct characteristics of each of the groups tends to be exaggerated in public attitudes and opinions about each group.

The Negroes and the foreign-born live in the same district, surrounding the high school in which the 1945 strikes originated. However, the foreign-born tend to consider this district a temporary home, to be left as soon as economic resources permit. The Negroes, on the other hand, are for the most part confined here by economic limitations and through unofficial real estate agreements. Very few Negro families have been able to buy property in any other sections of town.

Most public and religious activities are segregated. A

1. James H. Tipton, *Community in Crisis, The Elimination of Segregation from a Public School System* (New York: Bureau of Publications, Teachers College, Columbia University, 1953).

major problem for the city as a whole has been the segregation of city parks and beaches during the summer months.
This policy in the past led to racial tensions. The beaches are
bordered by a high-income white neighborhood, and local
opinion has been that these residents would object strongly
to unsegregated use of the beaches.

Gary's history of racial tensions and the flare-up of school
and racial disturbances in other Northern industrial cities in
the early 1940's led to the establishment of the Chamber of
Commerce Race Relations Committee in 1943 and the addition of Negro representatives to it in 1944. The labor unions
had an active educational program, as interracial in outlook
as their membership was in composition. Until the school
strikes began, the city had prided itself on its programs
designed to avoid racial difficulties.

The school strikes in Gary have been documented in James
H. Tipton's book, *Community in Crisis*. While interest here
centers in the period following the strikes, a short review of
the factors involved will be useful.

Unlike Cairo—where there was open resentment at the
influence of the NAACP which Cairo's citizens considered
an outside agency—the school strikes, or mass truancy, in
Gary appeared to have been instigated by one student in the
Froebel High School in September of 1945. Apparently it
was his desire to dramatize a tense situation which was the
catalyst leading to city-wide disturbances and disruption of
the schools for most of the school year. With the help of a
few classmates, he was able to lead an entire student body
out "on strike" because they claimed to object to having
Negro students in the school. For a short period, until the
school board and the administration agreed on a firm policy,
he held the center of the stage. As soon as the school administration agreed on and announced a firm policy of integrating
the schools, the strike leaders were encouraged to re-define
their aims and to take credit for a more democratic reason

for the mass truancy. Other community tensions which had found satisfactory outlet in aiding and abetting the truants were then focused on making the integrated system work.

Both the schools and the other community institutions were shocked into positive action in human relations as the result of the strikes. The schools embarked on an immediate integration program, a year before state legislation was passed.

Student integration began in September, 1947. It involved 116 Negroes who were placed in schools formerly for whites and the entire student bodies of two schools on the same site which were combined into one bi-racial school. The integration schedule called for a beginning in the first and sixth grades, with integration continuing in each successive grade each year following. This schedule was similar to that incorporated in the state law in 1949.

At Froebel High School, where the mass truancy originated, the exclusion of Negroes from the swimming pool and from the band was ended in 1947, but separate extra-curricular social organizations persisted. For example, there was a Senior Club and a Senior Organization composed, respectively, of whites and Negroes. It is planned that these will be abolished, but some teachers still cannot imagine a social function, such as a dance, without unpleasantness if both races attend. However, there have been no instances of bi-racial dating in this school.

At the present time segregation of students in the schools which are not bi-racial is almost entirely a function of residential segregation. The school districts have been drawn to approximate natural neighborhoods, and the children tend to go to the school nearest their homes. No transfers of white children out of home districts in order to avoid an integrated school have been permitted in recent years.

The school administration is still faced with a problem in regard to maladjusted Negro children in the integrated

schools, but, unlike some other communities, the school officials are aware of the problem and are trying to provide
remedial assistance for such youth. Retardation is also a
function of poverty and insecurity in the home environment.

Although there was one Negro teacher in the Froebel High
School in 1944 who was in charge of a class of "problem"
boys, the integration of faculties did not start as quickly as
that of students. By 1952 the proportion of Negro students
at Froebel had increased from 44 to 66 per cent, and the
Negro teachers represented 20 per cent of the faculty. The
Pulaski School, with 99 per cent of its students Negro, had
seven white teachers and forty-nine Negro teachers under
a Negro principal. In 1948 there were only two Negro
teachers outside the all-Negro Roosevelt School, but Negroes
now teach at two relatively new all-Negro elementary schools
and at Lincoln School where the proportion of Negro students has increased from 30 to 99 per cent since 1944.

Tension in the Gary schools has been reduced by the firmness of the school board and the administration, once a policy
of integration had been established. This reduction in tension
was first noticeable when the board persuaded the strike
leaders to change their demands completely from total *exclusion* of Negroes in the schools on strike to *inclusion* in these
and in all other schools in the city. The board has also
sponsored for the past five years an interracial city-wide
PTA, and it has been successful in eliminating the Parent
Teacher Organization, a dissident group of white parents
whose avowed purpose was the segregation of Negro children. Under school auspices, and with the assistance of
interested community organizations, workshops on human
relations have flourished. These provide teachers and school
administrators with training and with aids and techniques
for handling student problems in the integrated schools.

In addition there is a grade school organization called the
All-Out-Americans which works for intergroup understand-

ing. According to informed persons in the community this latter group is perhaps the most influential local organization in encouraging attitudes appropriate to a democratic school system in Gary. The AOA's, as they call themselves, include all the grade school children in both public and parochial schools, organized in each class, in each school, and city-wide. The AOA representatives work with other community leaders on community projects, such as the Red Cross and Community Chest drives, or in other activities requiring interracial support. The adult advisory board guides, but does not completely control, the juvenile group. The city-wide representatives meet monthly to discuss current problems. Representatives from schools for whites attend meetings at schools for Negroes, and Negro children meet at the schools attended by white children only. Parents in the advisory councils can observe the children functioning in interracial situations while they themselves share in these experiences. The aims of good citizenship, democracy, and service to school and community are stressed in this organization. Rewards for the children come through participation and in the form of parades and public recognition provided by the press and radio.

The sharp contrast between Gary and Cairo in the general public and official reactions to overt racial disturbance is obvious. Initial hesitancy was evident in both cities; but whereas Gary mobilized local leadership and gained control of the situation, in Cairo there was no evidence that, except for police protection of the minority at the height of the disturbance, any leadership was available from local officials or individual citizens. Gary mobilized community action in the interracial workshops; Cairo did not attempt to provide an atmosphere in which desegregated schools could function freely. It is unlikely that Gary would be caught unprepared should other trouble spots develop.

South Bend

Between 1940 and 1950 South Bend's population increased 14 per cent to 115,911 persons. At the same time its Negro population increased 129 per cent, from 3,555 to 8,134. This fact helps to explain why South Bend, which has never had segregated schools, appears to be moving in that direction. The schools have always served the residential district in which they are located. As they continue to do so, the slowly increasing size of the Negro residential sections, and the very rapid increase in the population within these areas, are forcing on the schools the racial concentrations and cleavages of the residential neighborhoods. This city thus illustrates the way in which housing segregation may become the basis for segregation in other community institutions.

The major center of Negro population is a rectangle west of the city center. It is bounded on the west by a buffer area of intermingled white and Negro homes, alleged to be designed to protect a development for upper middle-income whites on the western fringe of the city. Negroes are discouraged from buying property south of the main east-west thoroughfare.

Negroes now attend nineteen of the twenty-two public schools in the city, the exceptions being three elementary schools in districts where there are no Negroes. Between 1948 and 1952 the proportion of Negroes increased in most schools and greatly increased in two elementary schools. In one of these it went up from 80 per cent to 93 per cent. In the other it increased from 34 to 49 per cent. One school on the south side of the main thoroughfare does have a 50-50 proportion between the races, but this probably will soon be 25-75 per cent as a new school in a white neighborhood is being constructed somewhat farther removed from the sections in which Negroes are concentrated.

The proportion of Negroes in the high schools almost

doubled in the three year period ending in 1952, but it is still so low that segregation at this level is not a problem. One high school counted 15 per cent and another 17 per cent of its students from the Negro sub-community. A third had less than a dozen Negro students who felt that they were better off than their friends in the other schools because of greater social acceptance by the white students. Negroes are not excluded from any of the high school extra-curricular activities, including dances. However, white students reported that except for proms, few Negroes attended dances. Social clubs, which had excluded Negroes, have been banned in the schools.

The first Negro teacher in the public schools was hired in 1950, and there are now five, all at the school with the highest proportion of Negro students. There is also a Negro in the Office of Pupil Personnel. The stated policy of the school administration is to move slowly in the hiring of Negro teachers, using local people as much as possible.

One of the community leaders in intergroup relations was a principal at a high school who had done a great deal to foster harmonious relations within his school. All students were welcome at the noon-hour social period. All extra-curricular activities were interracial, including the use of the swimming pool. There was a tradition in this school that the vice-president of the senior class was a Negro. This school developed an SOS technique, through which teachers, social workers, and community leaders were alerted in the event of tension between the racial groups. They met at once, collected the facts of the incident, and tried to improve communication between the people involved in the misunderstandings.

Leadership has developed within the Negro community. Established families have helped immeasurably in introducing new arrivals to the ways of life in a Northern city. They have been active in the city-wide PTA and in other interracial groups. Without active and informed leadership in both groups and among city officials, South Bend might easily have been plagued with difficulties as were Gary and Cairo. In spite of a rapid increase in Negro population and some increase in segregated patterns, Negroes have been absorbed into community life with very little friction.

CHAPTER 7

Toward Integration:

CAMDEN, ATLANTIC CITY, BURLINGTON, AND SALEM, NEW JERSEY *

NEW JERSEY PROVIDES IN MICROCOSM A PICTURE OF MANY facets of race relations of the nation—the points of cleavage and agreement between Northern and Southern policies, the myriad variations in specific practices within each of these. For the present period of accelerated change in the basic patterns of public education in the nation, it is especially illuminating to look at the developments in a state where the interplay of social forces considered "Southern" and "Northern" are apparent, and where the lower half of the state has usually followed Southern traditions and customs (and in some cases, laws) in shaping its community life, particularly in those areas affecting elementary education.

New Jersey shares the strong American tradition of local responsibility and control in the public schools. Over four-fifths of the school funds come from the local communities. The salaries of school superintendents are fixed by local boards. School boards are reputed to act rather independently in their dealings with the State Department of Education. Furthermore, the way school boards are selected seems to influence strongly the extent of autonomy and the respon-

* Based on the report of field research prepared by John Hope II, Director of Industrial Relations, Race Relations Department, A.M.A., Fisk University.

siveness of the boards to the local people and the controlling
political leadership. Two systems are in use. In the so-called
Article 6 cities, board members are appointed by the mayor;
in other communities they are elected (Article 7 cities). In
the Article 7 cities, the school budget is voted on by the
electorate at the same time board members are elected. In
Article 6 cities the budget authority is exercised by a board
in which the mayor has a strong position to control policies.

While most of New Jersey is geographically above the
Mason-Dixon line, the history of its public school education,
especially at the elementary and junior high school levels, has
had more in common with states below than above this line.
In the southern counties both basic policies and prevailing
practices have been essentially similar to those of the Southern states. Before 1947 the sharp intersectional differences
between the policies and practices in the northern and
southern counties ran the complete gamut from total integration of both students and faculties to total segregation of
both. Nearly every conceivable kind of combination of the
two extremes has been found:

> . . . separate elementary and mixed junior and senior high
> schools; separate elementary and junior high schools and mixed
> high schools; divided buildings, one half for white and one half
> for Negroes; separate classes and teachers for each race within
> the same building; separate elementary schools for each race on
> the same school site; separate elementary schools joined by a
> common auditorium. In some instances the Negro children were
> taught by Negro teachers in the regular subjects and by white
> teachers in the special subjects. . . .[1]

These variations existed in spite of a law of 1881 nominally
prohibiting the exclusion of any child from any public school
on account of nationality, religion, or race. They illustrate

1. Marion Thompson Wright, *The Education of Negroes in New Jersey*
(New York: Bureau of Publication, Teachers College, Columbia University,
1941), pp. v-vi.

the fact that desegregation of schools has been a national rather than just a regional problem.

On the other hand, the study of New Jersey is unique in this series because it concerns the only state which instituted a system of integrated schools on a uniform, state-wide basis as the result of recent constitutional change (1948). For that reason, an examination of the total situation before and after 1948 should high-light some of the basic problems and the various solutions found to them.

The new constitution was approved by referendum in November, 1947, with the provision that it become effective January 1, 1948. Immediately after the opening of the New Jersey legislature in January, the commissioner of education assigned the task of implementation of the school desegregation provision to the Division Against Discrimination (DAD). The DAD had come into existence under New Jersey's Anti-Discrimination Law and had been operative in this field since 1945. The division's first move after being assigned the task of implementation was a complete survey of the public schools to determine to what extent, where, and how racial segregation was practiced.

A survey of sixty-two school districts, initiated in the spring of 1948, revealed that two-thirds had segregated schools sanctioned by local practice and custom. In an additional nine districts schools housing Negro pupils only were in operation, but according to the DAD this condition was the result of residential segregation rather than deliberate racial segregation in the school system itself. The pattern of segregation was concentrated in the elementary schools and to a lesser degree at the junior high school level. The fifty-two communities having segregated schools were in ten southern counties. Integration at the senior high school level was practically universal.

A comparison of the conditions throughout the state in 1947, the last year of accepted segregation, with 1952, shows many changes. In 1947 about 10 per cent of all school children in the state were Negro, and about 16 per cent of the Negro pupils were in segregated schools. In the ten southern counties where the segregated schools were located, Negroes constituted 5 per cent of the total school enrollment. Only 2 per cent of all teachers in the state were Negro, and most of them were in the segregated schools. The total school enrollment rose appreciably during this five-year period, with the larger increase in the southern counties. The number of teachers also increased, in about equal numbers in the two sections of the state. However, the number of school buildings decreased for the state as a whole and for the southern counties but increased in the northern counties. The tentative conclusion to be drawn from these data is that some excess school space was eliminated when desegregation allowed fuller use of existing facilities or allowed replacement of small rural schools with consolidated schools. The teacher load remained almost constant throughout the period, but the ratio of teachers and pupils to buildings increased.

Comprehensive information was not available on the size or change in capital investment during this period. However, state aid to local communities increased by one-fourth over the period, which probably indirectly indicates a growth in school facilities. This increase is significant because withholding of state aid was also a major punitive means available for use by the DAD in enforcing compliance with the law.

After 1948 many of the forty-three formerly segregated districts began using Negro teachers in bi-racial or in all-white classes for the first time. Some white teachers were placed in schools with a predominantly Negro student body. Qualified Negro teachers were assigned to high schools for the first time.

As shown later in this chapter, some communities were able in a short time to integrate the teaching staff without displacement of either white or Negro teachers. On the whole, the New Jersey experience did not bear out the fears that Negro teachers would be squeezed out of the schools or relegated to undesirable posts.

At least four methods were used to bring about integrated student bodies. First, two- to four-room schools were closed and the teachers and students reassigned to the remaining buildings. The dismissal of teachers with tenure was avoided by filling normal openings with the surplus teachers instead of hiring new ones. Those without tenure, both Negro and white, were in some instances dismissed. Fewer buildings to be maintained and fewer teachers to pay saved some communities appreciable sums of money. A second method of providing for desegregation involved the construction of new consolidated schools for a bi-racial enrollment; in these instances a number of small schools were closed over a two-year period. For example, in one community a modern building with five Negro and seven white teachers replaced ten one- and two-room buildings.

The third type of adjustment which was followed in several middle-sized communities was to transform the erstwhile schools for Negroes into intermediate or junior high schools with a bi-racial student body. Finally, in the larger towns and cities, school districts were rezoned and strict transfer regulations adopted, with the result that all children tended to go to the school nearest their homes.

How did the DAD implement the new constitution in the face of divergent practices and community sentiments? New Jersey boards of education enjoy a great deal of local autonomy because most of the school funds come from local real estate taxes. It has been estimated that state aid amounts to no more than 13 per cent of school funds. But this is usually the *marginal* amount needed by local boards. It therefore may have an especially strong impact upon the policies followed by local school boards. The DAD could have advised the withholding of state aid, but it felt that such a procedure might delay enforcement and engender bitterness in the local communities. Therefore the policy of the state agency was to make every effort to settle differences and bring about conformity through persuasion, conference, and conciliation. These friendly methods worked so well that by June, 1948, the DAD announced that twenty-two of the forty-three segregated districts had presented plans and announced publicly their intention to integrate completely pupils and teachers at the beginning of the school year in the fall. By September this number had risen to thirty. Nine other districts had presented partial plans or had taken measures to change the segregated arrangements by that date. In this latter group the boards of education were faced with the problem of actual building programs or of insufficient space, which made it difficult to bring about integration quickly. A few districts were definitely hesitant and favored gradualism over immediate integration. Of the four districts which made no plans, two denied that there was segregation, and two, in effect, repudiated the constitutional provision. The DAD thought that court hearings might be needed to bring these districts in line with the state law.

Experience up to this point revealed that there were three major types of segregation. First, some communities used gerrymandered school districts. Second, inconsistent bus routes in rural districts perpetuated the segregated schools. In the third place, school buildings were located in the middle of segregated housing areas and thus served only one race. Some of the segregated facilities were equal in plant and equipment; in others, the plant and equipment used by Negroes were substandard and could not be used in an integrated system.

In all the communities where a change in practice was involved, the boards of education had the responsibility of initiating the necessary directives and plans. They were the policy-making bodies at the local level, giving authority and guidance to the local school administration. The administrators had the responsibility for organizing an integration program. An examination of the means by which this was done indicated two major methods.

In the first pattern, the Board of Education established its local policy without participation from the public, parents, teachers, or students. It then advised the community of its plans and of the public roles and responsibilities, on the assumption that the plan would receive cooperation and support. Some communities followed the practice of making one formal announcement at the regular board meeting. Others held a series of meetings with the public *after* the board's plan had been completely formulated and approved. A few boards instructed the school officials to prepare a series of press releases followed up by a more formal statement to each child at the close of the school year.

In the second approach, the boards asked the community for some degree of participation in the actual formulation of local policy and solicited their acceptance of the policy before it was initiated. In some school districts, the boards held public meetings *before* any definite plans had been formulated. In others a gradual two-year plan was presented for local approval. These approaches to the problem did not appear to have been as effective as the first method described above. Public discussion and gradualism engendered some local resistance, aired divergent opinions, and gave time to focus public attention on purely administrative matters.

Since it was in the ten southern counties that resistances and varied practices were most evident, attention will be focused on them. In this chapter, four urban areas, three representing major industrial situations and one a more rural area, will be analyzed in some detail. The case of Mount Holly, where resistance appeared to be strong, will be discussed in Chapter 8. Camden and Burlington, in this chapter, represent urban areas of high industrial concentration along the Delaware River, contiguous to eastern Pennsylvania. Camden is the larger of the two, but Burlington is industrially significant. Atlantic City is the prototype of the resort area, its income largely derived from the tourist trade. The differences in employment opportunities are reflected in the occupational distributions of workers and in the community institutions and customs. Salem is a smaller industrial town surrounded by an agricultural area.

In these cities support of interracial agencies had been strong enough over a long enough period of time to facilitate immediate desegregation after the new constitution came into effect. For example, the NAACP for many years had carried out a persistent state-wide program. Its education committee was very active, conducting the survey of the state's school system and working closely with local NAACP branches. Such organizations as the NAACP had created effective procedures and local channels of communication for meeting the problems of integration. In many instances the interracial organizations had been sustained by, and in turn had helped to create, a substantial fund of good will among both white and Negro citizens. Local good will, however, became effective in achieving desegregation only when it secured the backing of the law.

Protest against the change was sporadic but handled quickly and conclusively, in spite of the fact that some school administrators themselves were not whole-heartedly in favor of the integrated system. Integration has not been total in either Camden or Atlantic City; residential segregation, location of existing school buildings, and the lack of districting in the elementary schools have limited what could be done immediately. Yet there is every indication that the administrators in these cities are trying to comply with the law and to make changes in accordance with it.

Camden

Camden, in contrast to such communities as New Albany and Jeffersonville, found that teacher integration was a useful procedure in desegregation where student bodies remained predominantly segregated. The city of Camden in 1950 had a population of 123,955 of which approximately 5.5 per cent was Negro. It is located in a larger metropolitan area, just across the Delaware River from Philadelphia. The industrial character of the city is indicated by the fact that two-thirds of the males are engaged in unskilled, semi-skilled, and skilled non-farm production; the major employment opportunities are in manufacturing, wholesale and retail trade, and construction.

The essential pattern of race relations is one of segregation except in those areas where state law has intervened since World War II. Important steps toward integration have occurred in the fields of employment and public school education, largely as a result of the application of the Anti-Discrimination Law of 1945, as later amended, and the public school desegregation requirements under the revised constitution of 1947. Such major employers as the New York Shipyards, Radio Corporation of America, Bell Telephone Company, and the Campbell Soup Company now hire Negroes for positions formerly held only by whites. One Negro leader observed that the problem now is to find qualified applicants for the new opportunities that are developing.

Generally speaking, places of public accommodation are officially open to Negroes on a non-segregated basis. Contrary action, in refusing service, is a violation of the Public Accommodations Act of 1949, termed the Freeman Amendment to the Anti-Discrimination Act of 1945. Private social and religious organizations, in general, continue to be segregated. The YMCA opened a new branch for Negroes recently; the

YWCA has accepted Negroes on an integrated basis only in the last few years.

The pattern of housing, both public and private, is generally segregated. The main Negro residential area approximates a mid-town ghetto, but there are also some scattered segregated areas outside this central district. There are a few blocks of mixed occupancy here and there. In a large city where residential segregation on the basis of race is the rule and where the schools have been located to meet the needs of a segregated educational system, it is difficult to rezone the school districts to eliminate the most obvious inequalities. Parents of both races may be dissatisfied and critical of whatever changes the school administration makes. This was one of the first problems of the Camden School Board in complying with the new constitution.

The school districts in use in 1947 were deemed obsolete since they had been operative at least as far back as 1931. The school board directed that they be redrawn on the basis of nearness to school; after that was done, in some instances the boundaries were "bent" to meet the most serious dissatisfactions arising in small fringe groups. Once the new districts were announced, the next administrative step was to see that the transfer privilege was not used to defeat the integration goal. That it was so used, through guardian addresses, will be discussed later.

Some persons interviewed in this study held that the Camden Board of Education was not in favor of desegregation during the early transition. Since 1944 the local branch of the NAACP had been meeting with the board at intervals, asking that some of the schools be desegregated. Nothing was accomplished until after the revised state constitution went into effect. Some said that during the first year of the process of desegregation, the board was accused of being too lenient with transfer privileges, but most informants agreed that after the initial stages, the policy of refusing transfers on the basis of race alone was more uniformly enforced. Allegations of quiet avoidance of the full implications of an integrated system seem to be an inevitable part of the transition period, whatever the overt actions of a local board.

The position of the school authorities was that they were complying with the law as speedily as they deemed wise in the interests of the children involved. The NAACP, on the other hand, was of the opinion that in some instances the board was unduly hesitant and that it could have moved faster without endangering the end results.

During the school year 1947-1948 the school administration took the initiative in formulating plans for the change in policy and from that time forward did not lose control of the situation. This orientation was primarily to the school itself, rather than to the impact of the change on community sentiment. A special committee from the public school system was appointed to study the segregated schools and make recommendations as to how the practice could best be eliminated. It also appropriated funds to send three teachers (two white and one Negro) to the Rutgers University Workshop on Human Relations during the summer of 1948. These teachers were selected carefully by the superintendent and given the responsibility of returning with as many suggestions as possible on aids, techniques, and methods of integration.

An extension course on "Foundations of Human Relations" was given during the school year 1947-1948, and teachers were encouraged to attend. The course met weekly for two hours throughout the year, and it was well attended. In this way the faculties of the different schools were prepared for the desegregated situation and to assist in student adjustments the following year.

Some overt resistance gained short-lived notoriety in the fall of 1948. The parents of some fifteen white students objected to having their children transferred to what had been a school for Negroes only. The children in question lived on the edge of a new school district, adjacent to the Negro neighborhood, and the new district line put them in the former school for Negroes. After consultations, the board agreed that these children could continue that phase of their education in the school in which they had started it but that new entrants should attend the rezoned school.

Informed persons stated that during the first year of the process, both Negro and white parents transferred their children outside their proper districts by using "guardian addresses" of persons living elsewhere for no reason other than to avoid the desegregated schools. This use of the transfer privilege was soon halted, and there is no evidence that it is an important factor in the school situation today.

An instance of substantial protest appeared in one school where a Negro principal was appointed. The majority of the students were white—children from a low-income Italian-American neighborhood. The day before the school term began, a number of parents appeared at the principal's office to protest his appointment and request transfers for their children. Fifteen pupils, about 18 per cent of the enrollment, withdrew to a parochial school. By mid-term, however, according to the school administration reports, the principal had become so popular with both students and parents that all except three of those who withdrew returned to this school. This principal was known for his exceptional interest in the welfare of the children in his school.

Some tangible results of the desegregation process are shown in the following facts. In 1947 there were twenty-five elementary schools that were attended mainly by white children only (thirteen of these had no Negro pupils at all) and eight used exclusively by Negroes. In 1953, there were only ten schools which had no Negro pupils and only two in which there were no whites. In the elementary schools formerly for Negroes the relative out-flow was greater than the in-flow of Negroes into the schools predominantly for whites. In the junior and senior high schools the proportion of Negro students remained roughly constant from 1947 to 1953. During this period the number of elementary schools was reduced from thirty-three to twenty-nine as a result of the closing of one Negro and three white schools. The board was able to effect this financial saving because the desegregated situation allowed more economical use of the available facilities.

During a period of nearly constant enrollment, 1945-1951, the average teaching load, number of teachers per building, and number of pupils per building remained virtually constant, i.e., about 27 students per teacher, 16 teachers per building, and 416 pupils per building. From 1947 to 1953 the percentage of total capacity used in the schools predominantly for whites increased from 73 to 89 per cent; utilization increased in 17 of these elementary schools, remained constant in one, and decreased in only 4. In the schools formerly for Negroes the degree of utilization decreased from 80 to 73 per cent.

Perhaps even more indicative of the change in policy was the hiring of Negro teachers at the high school level and in supervisory capacities. There were no Negro teachers in the high school before 1945, but by 1951 there were eight, two of whom were teaching in the senior high school. The number of Negro principals increased from four to five, while the number of white principals remained at twenty-four. Two of the Negro principals had supervision of integrated faculties in 1951. Between 1945 and 1951 the number of Negro elementary teachers increased from eighteen to ninety-six. The extent of integration of Negro teachers throughout the Camden Public School System during the period of transition was more pronounced than that of pupils.

In addition to the board's policy of hiring teachers on the basis of qualifications without regard to race, other factors seem to have operated to increase the number and proportion of Negro teachers in the Camden school system. The integration process was begun at a period of acute teacher shortage which worked to the advantage of the qualified Negro teachers who had not been accepted until that time. In this same period, however, the range of alternative job opportunities for white women was much broader and the salary scales more attractive than was the teacher salary scale. Camden paid its teachers less than did surrounding urban school systems, and it is possible that the neighboring cities drew some white teachers from the Camden system. These factors apparently made teaching in the Camden system more attractive for Negroes than for whites. After the board realized that its apprehensions about using Negroes in the integrated situation were unfounded, they were also more willing to consider the applications of qualified Negro teachers.

As a result of these factors influencing the hiring and reassignment of teachers, Negroes were given bi-racial classes, and in some cases they were assigned to schools having very few, if any, Negro pupils. Negro students went to schools previously for whites, and some white students and teachers were in schools that were formerly for Negroes. However, the latter movement was very slight.

Criticism of the initial stages of the desegregation process stemmed mostly from those who had hoped to see it move faster and involve the entire school personnel quickly. The board found that it was easier and simpler to move Negro teachers and students into formerly white schools than to reverse the process. The first Negro teachers appointed to desegregated classes were selected carefully on the basis of superior qualities and adaptability. It was alleged by some local people that these teachers were given no choice in assignment but that the white teachers were canvassed to see if they would accept such assignments. This is a recurring complaint of differential treatment and a very sore point with Negro teachers. Unless a school board announces a firm policy on this point, it is likely to remain a sensitive subject.

During the first year, Negro as well as white teachers expressed some reluctance about assignments in the desegregated schools. The Negro teachers were generally apprehensive as to whether they would be accepted by their colleagues and the pupils, whereas the whites sometimes reacted through deep-seated prejudices against the other race rather than through fear of a new situation. Thus, while the resistance on the part of Negro teachers was relatively short-lived, that of the whites did in some instances persist. With this in mind, the administration tried to select teachers from new applicants who were not inclined to refuse any assignment or from teachers whose experience and training in interracial matters fitted them for such assignments. In some instances teachers who were not outstanding but who had tenure were given the alternative of this type of assignment or of becoming full-time substitute teachers. That selection on the basis of fitness through training is the method most likely to be successful seems borne out by the experience here.

The experience of Camden illustrates some of the administrative problems involved in the initial stages. The first efforts of the school administration were two-fold: the obsolete school districts had to be rezoned, while at the same time the administrators had to be on the alert to possible misuse of the transfer privilege. Concurrently, the faculties and administrative staffs of the schools were being encouraged to take special training in intergroup relations so that they would be prepared to assist their students in adjusting to a new situation. In cases where residential segregation limited what could be done toward integrating the student body, the administrators found that integrated faculties served to broaden the horizons of the students involved and that there was little objection on the part of the parents in the community. If the board's solutions did not fully satisfy the more aggressive groups in the community, they did serve to keep organized resistance at a minimum.

Atlantic City

Atlantic City is a prototype of resort areas, rendering a wide variety of services to vacationers and convention groups. These services furnish employment to the greater part of the labor force of the city. Almost 25 per cent of the employed males work in hotels or lodging houses or render personal service to these places. Another 25 per cent are employed by the various retail establishments. Only about 6 per cent of the male employed persons are in manufacturing, as compared to over 40 per cent in Camden in 1950.

Occupationally the resort character of the community is reflected in the 35 per cent who were service workers outside of private households, in contrast to just over 8 per cent in Camden. Less than one-third of the male employed workers were skilled and semi-skilled in Atlantic City, while over half of those in Camden were in these categories. Atlantic City lives by its service to the out-of-town guests from all parts of the country. In the field of race relations the segregated pattern of the hotels and restaurants had changed, as it had in Cincinnati. Part of the pressure for change came from convention groups with bi-racial personnel, part came as a result of the Anti-Discrimination Law. Now these services are at least nominally available on an unsegregated basis to all races, and proprietors' fears of loss of patronage have not been borne out.

Before 1945, the pattern of race relations was one of general segregation, and for the indigenous population this is still true. The most rapid changes have occurred in the services rendered to strangers, to the tourist trade. The exception to this statement lies in the realm of school administration, where there have been interracial committees and conferences for some years. The atmosphere of the city does not indicate that there is serious tension between Negroes and whites.

Employment for Negroes on the city pay roll has been limited to police and teachers; there has been no representation on the City Council. In private employment Negroes have been concentrated in the more menial jobs in the service trades. Service occupations characterize 44 per cent of Negro men and 68 per cent of Negro women; among whites the corresponding figures are 11 and 22 per cent. However, the proportions of whites and Negroes employed as "operatives and kindred workers" are practically identical.

Housing, both public and private, is as completely segregated as in most Southern communities, and with almost no exceptions, efforts of Negroes to buy property outside of Negro sections have been fruitless. The Negro population lives in a densely settled residential area to the north of the city center. The expansion of this area has been westward toward the marshes, as the proportion of Negroes in Atlantic City increased. This sharp division of the white and Negro residential areas posed many problems for the school administration in its efforts to desegregate the schools.

Atlantic City illustrates clearly that the personal attitudes of school administrators may influence the speed, if not the direction, of change. During the transition period, from 1947 to 1950, there were three different city school superintendents and at least two different points of view represented among them. All these men operated under the same basic Board of Education, but the policies varied with the superintendent.

At the time the new constitution went into effect, the superintendent and the Board of Education decided upon the policies and regulations which they deemed appropriate for the implementation of the state law. The schools had been operated under the principle that any child might attend the school of his choice, provided there was room for him. This principle is still being followed. In contrast to Camden and many other communities, the board not only did not fix clearly defined zones and boundary lines but indicated that there were no mandatory boundaries. This was not announced as a policy until the fall of 1948 when pressure from the NAACP and individual Negro citizens resulted in a public announcement.

In 1948 a committee was appointed to study ways and means of implementing the state law within the framework of the local "school of choice" rule. According to the DAD files, this committee studied the problem from several angles and presented various plans, but none of them was regarded by the DAD as satisfactory. Little shift in the student population took place under the administration of the first superintendent.

When the desegregation program went into effect, it was technically true that the elementary grades were legally desegregated because of the "school of choice" rule. However, there were practical difficulties which prevented Negro children from attending the schools for whites. The schools for whites are in the southern part of the city, those for Negroes in the northwest. Distances and traffic hazards were too great for many small Negro children to be able to go to the schools for whites, with the exception of two which were nearer the center of town and thus closer to the Negro neighborhoods. Negro students in junior high school continued to be segregated, even under the board's ruling, since they were almost all in the two schools for Negroes.

The following year a new superintendent took office for one year. In the fall of 1950 the junior high schools and one elementary school were integrated. The total school population as of July, 1950, was: elementary schools, 60 per cent white and 40 per cent Negro; junior high school, 66 per cent white and 34 per cent Negro; and senior high school, 80 per cent white and 20 per cent Negro.

In the conference at the end of the school year, 1949-1950, the Atlantic City school administration made certain commitments to the DAD for increasing further the degree of integration of students. The DAD and the commissioner of education were considering withholding state aid should the situation not show more improvement. The local administration did not favor any form of districting for the existing elementary schools in the city, because it felt that the peculiar location of these buildings meant that integration would not be promoted by this method. However, it planned school additions wherever building extensions would lend themselves to program integration. For example, one school at that time had a 50-50 population as between white and Negro students, but the white students were gradually leaving the school partly, it was thought, because it did not offer the variety of courses and activities found in the other schools. The administration planned improvements and new teacher appointments to make this a more attractive school. This was done, but the results were not as hoped for. By 1953, only 10 per cent of the students were white. "School of choice" gave white students the opportunity to retreat to more distant schools with a lower ratio of Negro students.

The second commitment to the DAD was a shift from the 6-2-4 to the 6-3-3 school plan on the ground that the latter was both more economical and could be planned in such a way as to further promote the spirit as well as the letter of the desegregation law. The administration also committed itself to handle the transferring of students in accord with the law. Where student bodies are still predominantly of one race, the present administration has placed teachers of the opposite race as a means of educating the children in interracial relations. The present superintendent has also created incentives for all teachers to keep up in their fields by attaching salary increments for specific study and advancement. Teachers said his standards were more objective than those which had existed formerly.

The established patterns of professional relations of teachers may have been an important factor in the absence of friction that has characterized the desegregation process. Teacher meetings were held on a completely integrated basis for some years, and joint participation of white and Negro teachers as committee members was commonplace. In addition, joint participation of student groups from segregated schools was encouraged in a variety of activities before 1947. Negro and white teachers and staff members participated on an integrated basis in their respective professional organizations for many years, and Negroes served as officers in these groups.

However, these interracial organizations and the study of the problems surrounding race relations apparently did not contribute much to the speed of desegregation. It is generally agreed by local informants that without the authority of state legislation, desegregation would not have moved as fast if it could have been accomplished at all. It is also true that although the Negro members of the professional organizations had been officers at times in the past, none had been elected to top executive positions until after 1948. Several of these persons had been active in the organizations for years.

Efforts of Negroes, through such organizations as the NAACP and of individual parents through the courts, to eliminate segregation in the schools far antedate 1947. The schools also had made surveys of the teachers to get their reactions on the problem and to focus attention on the need for its consideration. Educational techniques for evaluating and improving human relations were highly developed in this city, but sufficient specific motivation to break with tradition was lacking until the legal change of 1947.

There was little evidence of community tension at the various stages of the desegregation process. No special preparations were made for inaugurating the various steps or for elevating Negro teachers to higher levels in the system. The Board of Education simply announced the appointment of teachers as the occasion warranted.

That community attitudes and fears other than those directly related to education may influence the citizens in their evaluation of the school program is a factor which sometimes has to be considered by the school administration. For example, a Negro family managed to purchase some property in the middle of a white section of town. Immediately the white parents of the neighborhood began to protest to the school administration. Their point was that the initiation of the 6-3-3 plan at this time would allow Negro children in the junior high school in the vicinity and would "threaten" the neighborhood, decreasing property values. The superintendent and the Board of Education stood firm on the announced changes, and no further disturbances were noted.

The significance of this new plan is apparent from the positions of the two new junior high schools and the rigid boundaries of the zones which determine school attendance. The new boundary was drawn some three blocks further north than the former line to insure a balanced enrollment and an integrated student body. This districting facilitated the equitable use of existing buildings and resulted in considerable monetary savings. Such zoning is possible at the secondary school level without handicapping the students who normally travel greater distances to and from school than do elementary pupils.

A comparison of the methods used in Cincinnati with those employed in Atlantic City in dealing with the rezoning of school districts may throw some light on the possible effects of different techniques. It will be recalled that in Cincinnati two school districts were drawn in such a way that children were kept in the school nearest their homes and that, at the time, this made both schools all-Negro in composition. In Atlantic City, on the other hand, the argument was advanced that districting would only perpetuate segregation.

Yet under the "school of choice" principle in Atlantic City, there are specific school situations which tend to contradict the statement that districting favors segregation. In the two schools nearest the Negro neighborhoods, there was a marked tendency for white children to withdraw to more distant schools as the proportion of Negro children increased, thus in effect turning these into schools for Negroes. While the schools still had a bi-racial student body, the proportion of white children decreased without a noticeable change in the total enrollment. Had these schools been districted this could not have happened even though zoning would have kept other elementary schools segregated. Another argument advanced for districting was that there still were very few Negro children in the schools in the southern sections of the city; the "school of choice" rule allowed the school administration to respond to any protesting parents that all schools were open if there was room for the child.

In contrast to Camden's rather widespread dispersion of Negro pupils among elementary schools formerly for whites, almost no pupil integration at this level has taken place in Atlantic City. Of the eight "white" schools, four have remained exclusively white; only a few Negroes are found in two others, and one is rapidly shifting from a white to a Negro school through the exodus of white pupils.

In spite of the "retreat" of some white students from integregated schools, those who remained, particularly in the junior and senior high schools, appeared to participate fully on an integrated basis in all school sponsored activities. Relations between Negro and white students have been harmonious. One school official felt that probably the most satisfying and fundamental result of the integration process was the evidence of "change in the heart" of the students and people generally, from "quota thinking" to the acceptance of the individual without regard to race. He cited school elections as an example; in one school in which the student body was about 80 per cent white and 20 per cent Negro, three Negro and two white students were elected to serve on the youth commission recently. Apparently the vote reflected judgment of individual abilities without regard to race. However, in undirected leisure activities, school officials still noted a tendency for student groups to separate along racial lines.

That the present administration is genuinely attempting to promote integration is shown by its record on teacher assignments. In 1947 the first Negro teacher was assigned to the Technical High School. The following year a Negro teacher was moved to the elementary school which had a bi-racial student body. With the beginning of the present administration, four white teachers were placed in schools for Negroes, two Negro teachers were appointed to the high school, and special teachers in such subjects as music and art were assigned without regard to race or color and moved freely from school to school. In addition, two more Negroes were placed in integrated classes during this year. When the Negro junior high school students were transferred to the Central Junior High School in 1950-1951, ten of their teachers were also assigned to this school.

From the point of view of the Negro teachers, a milestone was passed when, in 1951, three teachers were transferred from the junior to the senior high school. For the first time, the school administration was making appointments of Negro teachers on the basis of their highest qualifications. At least two of the three so assigned had all of the necessary qualifications for certification as high school teachers when they entered the public school system some fifteen years previously, but at that time they could not be placed above the primary level because of discriminatory restrictions.

There has been a planned program of placing teachers of the opposite race in schools predominantly of one race to introduce Negro teachers into schools where there are few Negro students. It was the opinion of the administration that this has worked exceptionally well and has had the approval of both faculty and students. According to one administrator, the success of this type of assignment depends on avoiding an increase in the number of Negroes beyond that which is considered prudent and expedient in the light of the community situation at the time.

In the integrated situations, particularly in junior and senior high schools, there appeared to be full participation of Negroes in all school sponsored activities, and relations were considered harmonious. One high school teacher expressed the view that the efforts of the principal and teachers to see that Negroes were not left out of any school activities did much to eliminate some racial tensions which had been noticed from time to time before there was teacher as well as student integration in this school.

The promotion of Negro teachers to positions which utilize fully their qualifications without regard to the racial composition of the classes they teach is an important qualitative change in the Atlantic City school system. The total number of teachers has remained practically constant during this period, as has the Negro share in teacher assignment. At the same time, the proportion of Negro students has increased, and the teaching load increased from thirteen to twenty-two. The average number of teachers per building increased from almost seventeen to twenty as the result of the closing of one school and converting two elementary schools into junior high schools. The number of pupils per building also rose from 223 to 421 for the same reasons. It seems evident that there was considerable "excess" building space under a dual system of education and also that there may have been an excess of teachers. Atlantic City had one of the two lowest teaching loads among the New Jersey communities studied.

Burlington

Burlington illustrates a situation in which recently improved facilities in schools for Negroes can be used for bi-racial student populations. Burlington County has grown more rapidly than the state as a whole during the past decade. In the city of Burlington in 1950, there were 10,093 persons, of whom almost 19 per cent were Negro. For the county as a whole the Negro population amounted to only 9 per cent. Roughly one-fourth of the male workers in this city were classified as craftsmen, foremen, and kindred workers; almost 30 per cent as operators and 13 per cent as non-farm laborers. The median number of school years completed for the residents of Burlington was 8.5.

Burlington is an old, settled community where there were Negro families before the War between the States. Descendants of these families take great pride in their long association with the city. There were increases in the Negro population during each of the world wars, the most recent involving the hiring of Negroes as laborers by the U.S. Type and Foundry Company.

As in the other New Jersey communities, important changes in the range of employment opportunities have occurred since 1948. Some stores have hired Negroes in other than menial jobs, as have some city departments, but these changes so far have affected very few people. Housing is segregated but not in the ghetto formation; there are small settlements of Negroes in several neighborhoods in the city. Social and religious organizations are segregated. Negroes and whites use the same facilities at the YMCA, but in separate groups.

Before September, 1948, the Burlington public school system consisted of a high school, a junior high school for seventh and eighth grades, and five elementary schools. Two of the latter were for Negroes, staffed by a Negro principal and nine teachers. Just before 1948, about a dozen Negro children had been admitted to the school for whites nearest their homes.

Informed persons in the community reported that before the present school administration came into office, the facilities for the two schools for Negroes were definitely inferior to the schools for whites. One of the first tasks of this administration was to attempt to make all facilities, services, and salaries equal. That this effort already had been started made the complete integration process somewhat easier than it might otherwise have been.

School administrators pointed out that in this community there was a significant difference between the expression of personal feelings of individuals and the assumption of their civic responsibilities as school officials. Some members of the city council and of the school board were personally opposed to integration, but they voted unanimously in favor of it in their official capacities. There was at the time a Negro member of the board.

The specific steps taken by the city to bring about complete integration were significant. Shortly after the revised state constitution went into effect the school officials held a conference with a representative of the State Department of Education and asked if a directive was to be sent to each county from the state office. The local officials thought that such action might have strengthened their position and transferred some of the "onus of desegregation" from the local staff to the more distant state agency. When informed that no such directive would be issued, the local board met and selected a citizens' committee "to study the segregation of the public school students in the City of Burlington." The committee was asked to review the problems facing the local community and to recommend to the board procedures for the elimination of segregation. When the committee reported to the board, the superintendent submitted a memorandum to the Board of Education. He stated that in view of the findings of the committee, it was his recommendation that complete desegregation of the students and staff be made at once, starting in the fall of 1948.

The citizens' committee, which had been chosen to represent many facets of city life, met again to approve the proposed recommendation for desegregation. It gave the school board authority to use its name for publicity where needed. It was the policy of the board to do no more than inform the community that the board was acting under the directive of the new constitution. They felt that friction and dissent would be minimized in this way.

The administrative techniques of desegregation included rezoning the entire city. Every elementary school principal made a map showing where each child in his school lived. From these maps new attendance areas were drawn, based on the location of students and capacity of buildings. The board then approved the new districts and announced them in the newspapers. It also agreed not to authorize any transfers from one district to another when transfers would be means to avoid desegregation.

Letters were sent to all parents before the close of the school year, informing them of the constitutional provision and advising them which school each child would attend the following year. On the last day of school, every child who was to be transferred was taken to his new school for a visit, orientation, and a talk. The children met their new teachers and classmates before the summer vacation started. This procedure is in marked contrast to practices followed in most of the other communities studied.

The process of integrating the faculties was also studied

carefully. The superintendent had conferences with all principals, asking their cooperation in putting the best qualified teachers in the most integrated class rooms. He felt that children should have the opportunity to meet the "finest representatives" of the white and Negro teachers in this initial period. The teachers were informed of their new assignments on the same day that the children were so that there would be no wild rumors. No teachers, white or Negro, were given the right to accept or reject the new assignment. This, too, is in marked contrast to the more usual procedure of giving white teachers preference in assignments.

There were no organized protests from faculty or students. The superintendent was criticized at first by some white adults who felt that the board was moving faster than necessary. It was noted that near-by communities, such as Mount Holly, were not going all the way in the program, and the local officials were accused of "rushing in" while there was still a chance of avoiding the issue if the community would just "sit tight and get away with doing nothing." Some citizens, less opposed to integration, still felt that the board's action might defeat a school building program that was being put before the voters during the 1949 school year. However, the cooperation of the citizens' committee and other interested groups helped to pass the school building project without difficulty.

In the elementary schools the proportion of Negro to white students varies from 25 to 75 per cent, depending on the residential pattern surrounding the school. The Negro teachers already in the system were retained, and one of them was assigned to a school in an upper middle-class white neighborhood. Mild protest was registered at this, but within a few months she was being invited home with her students for lunch. No Negro teachers have yet been assigned to the junior or senior high schools.

Burlington had some serious problems because it was not

in a position to close any of its school buildings and thus eliminate movement of white children to erstwhile schools for Negroes. This created some short-lived tension among the white residents. However, the advance planning and careful publicity to parents eased possible conflict. In other communities studied, the student movement has been toward the schools for whites.

In this city where almost a fifth of the population was Negro, the leadership of the superintendent of schools, and the confidence in his judgment displayed by the Board of Education and the community at large, made the transition from a segregated to a desegregated situation a smooth and relatively effortless one. Apparently, not only did the community gain in interracial understanding, but the school system was able to effect some savings in school costs by more equitable use of available equipment. Initial fears of Negro teachers that they would not have the same opportunities for advancement or for new appointments have not been justified nor have the fears expressed by some members of the board that the superintendent would "pack" the faculties with Negroes. It is true that teachers are now hired on the basis of qualifications alone and that in some instances Negroes have been hired when there were also white applicants for the position.

Several interviews with white students reinforced the impression gained from the opinions of informed adults that the adjustment of the children to the new situation was relatively uncomplicated by racial considerations. The teachers were said to be accepted for their own qualities, and several of the Negro teachers were reported to be outstandingly successful in the integrated classes. Eighth grade pupils were asked to write an autobiography telling which teacher had most influenced them. One Negro teacher was most often named. She was described by informants as a rather dark-skinned person who had, during her first year in the desegregated school, been very fearful of her ability to function well there. However, she was sought out by both parents and colleagues when her pleasant personality became known. Parents said that while she was not the most perfect disciplinarian, she gave the children an appreciation of courtesy, respect, and the value of the social graces. Other Negro teachers were also praised for their ability to stimulate students in their work and for encouraging them in community projects.

Burlington, with Tucson, Arizona, and Elkhart, Indiana, illustrate a situation in which the integration of the public schools was accepted easily and one in which the experience in the schools may have a lasting effect in the relations between the races in the community at large.

Salem

Salem, like some other communities to be described later, has succeeded in operating desegregated schools in spite of community sentiments which would be expected to support rigid segregation. The city of Salem is perhaps the most "Southern" in its general atmosphere of any New Jersey community studied. It is located in the southwestern part of the state, with close ties to Maryland and Delaware. In 1950 the population of the county was 49,508, of whom 14 per cent were Negro. However, in the city itself 26 per cent of the total of 9,050 were Negro. Over half of the city workers were in manufacturing, particularly pottery, and another 16 per cent in the retail trades.

Salem does not have a sharply segregated pattern of housing. In the older sections of town it is common to find a Negro home at the back of a white dwelling. This housing pattern was started before the War between the States when the town was very sympathetic to the institution of slavery. However, it also had a strong Quaker settlement which was known to assist runaway slaves. These dual influences persist at the present time.

Until very recently, Salem was a completely segregated town except for the high school. Restaurants would not serve Negroes; Negroes were required to sit in the balcony at theaters and other public places, and they were either excluded or segregated in other places of public accommodation. Even after 1948, when a convention of a Negro organization met in Salem, some white restaurants closed to avoid having to serve Negroes. Others, serving them, were discourteous and slow in service.

Since 1948, there has been some reduction of restrictions on Negroes in public accommodations. One mill sometimes hires Negroes above the level of unskilled labor, and the police department has begun hiring Negroes as patrolmen.

Just before the desegregation of the schools, there were over 9,000 pupils in the public schools of the whole of Salem county, of whom 9 per cent were Negroes in the segregated schools and 5 per cent Negroes in integrated schools. In Salem City, of the total public school population of 1,881 in 1947, 11 per cent were Negroes in segregated and 4 per cent were Negroes in unsegregated schools. There was no segregation in high school, but two adjacent elementary schools were segregated. One housed Negro children from kindergarten through eighth grade, and it was staffed by eight teachers, one of whom was a teaching principal.

The year before desegregation was required, the seventh and eighth grade children were moved into a desegregated junior high school. This change was made because of overcrowding in the lower grades. At the same time, two Negro teachers were placed in the high school building in charge of bi-racial classes at the junior high school level.

The school administration had the cooperation of the Board of Education throughout the desegregation process. It was the board's policy to establish the means for bringing about integration and then simply announce that it had been done according to voter mandate. This announcement was made in the spring of 1948. No citizens' committee was formed, and there was no public discussion with either teachers or students. It seems to have been the opinion of the administrators that the less said the better.

The administrative steps used were different from any encountered in the other communities studied. Since the schools use homogeneous groupings, rated according to ability, all students in each of the two groups rated were listed by grade on individual slips of paper and each grade put in a separate container. There were no racial designations on the slips. Late in August each teacher was asked to draw her quota of students from the appropriate container. This method was used so that not even the teacher would know until just before school opened whether she had Negro students in her class.

A few days before the term opened, the newspaper announced which schools would house each of the primary grades. On opening day, the children were directed to their home rooms and learned who their teacher and classmates would be. The board agreed with the school administration that no transfers would be allowed. The administration was able to tell all parents that the method of assigning teachers and pupils had been random and that there was no favoritism shown.

The Negro teachers were integrated into all three of the elementary schools. In one the Negro teacher-principal remained as principal with five white teachers on his staff. One Negro teacher who was certified at that level was placed in the junior high school.

Several factors facilitated the school's task. In the first place, there were no school districts because the community was relatively small. In the second place, there was no sharply segregated residence pattern to complicate the process. Then, too, the Negro teachers in the system had been stable members of the community for a number of years and were respected by those who knew them. The superintendent carefully selected the white teachers who were to work under the Negro principal, but he gave them no choice of assignment. All those who were selected to teach bi-racial classes accepted their assignments and are reported to have worked well in this school.

From these four New Jersey communities—Camden, Atlantic City, Burlington, and Salem—some points of similarity and difference may be drawn, as well as some assessment made of the administrative procedures used.

All were operating under a clear, unequivocal state directive which removed the possibility of effective hedging on desegregation itself. Each had a history of well-developed community interest in, and support for, intergroup agencies and human relations studies. All except Salem had the problem of residential segregation which complicated the school administration's problems with desegregation. Unlike some of the other communities studied, there seemed to be a genuine interest in the personal problems of adjustment facing the Negro and white students and teachers in the new situation, and each community seemed to try to take these personal relations into account as its policies and programs were planned.

Of the administrative practices developed, well-defined districts and clear-cut transfer rules seemed most effective both for desegregation and for operating efficiency. The practice of placing Negro teachers in schools in which the student body remained predominantly white apparently was well received by both racial groups. Careful selection of teachers for the transition period—but without giving individual teachers the choice of accepting or refusing assignments—seemed to reduce tension and to increase the feeling that assignments were made on the basis of teaching qualifications only. For a small community such as Salem, the random distribution of students appeared to keep to a minimum complaints about individual favoritism or discrimination. That the desegregation directive ran counter to the individual preferences of many people did not keep it from being used effectively in each of the communities, nor did it decrease official support even by some individuals who were not themselves strongly in favor of it.

PART III

Desegregation Permitted

CHAPTER 8

Initial Hesitation:
PHOENIX, DOUGLAS, AND NOGALES, ARIZONA; MOUNT HOLLY, NEW JERSEY *

MOVING FROM NEW JERSEY TO THE SOUTHWEST, DESEGREGA-
tion appears in a different legal and social context. In Arizona the permissive nature of the 1951 state law left the
decision on integration up to the local school authorities.
This chapter will focus on the resistances, their basis in fact
and fiction, and their diminution in a short time.

However, the pattern illustrated in Arizona is a social, not
a geographic, fact. Bracketed with Arizona, therefore, is a
community in New Jersey, Mount Holly. Even under a mandatory law this community developed what seemed to be
intractable resistance to desegregation. Both Phoenix and
Mount Holly appeared to contain strong resistance to desegregation, but each moved rather quickly to desegregate.
In Douglas and Nogales, the process was slow but not so
obviously resisted.

Phoenix

Phoenix, the largest city in Arizona, is the center of an
area of intensive agriculture in the southwestern desert. The

* Based on the report of field research prepared by Edward and Marianna
Dozier, Northwestern University; and John Hope II, Fisk University.

city proper had a population of 105,000 in 1950, of whom approximately 15 per cent were Negro. The greater Phoenix area, however, counted 225,000 persons. Somewhat less than half of the population is of Spanish-American extraction, and in addition there are some 2,000 Indians living away from reservations.

A large proportion of the Anglo-American population of Phoenix is of Southern background. Phoenix residents often describe their community as conservative. It is the shopping center for the surrounding farm area, and wealth in the city is derived from commerce, agriculture, horticulture, and livestock.

The intricacies of the Phoenix public school system must be recognized to understand in part the difficulties the city faced when a desegregated school system was proposed. Within the greater Phoenix area there are twelve separate, independent elementary school districts, each with its own superintendent and three-member board of education. The high school district is another separate administrative unit encompassing the area of the twelve elementary districts but with its own superintendent and five-member board. By the nature of the Negro residential pattern only two elementary school districts were greatly involved in desegregation; a third district had a few Negro residents. The high schools, of course, were vitally concerned with the problem.

In the greater Phoenix area there are four main settlements of Negroes, all south of the center of the city. Three of these comprise most of one school district, with the fourth in a different district. There is some intermingling of Spanish-American and Negro populations in these districts. A very few Negroes live in Anglo-American neighborhoods.

Although Negroes are discriminated against in jobs, public accommodations, restaurants, and the like, some changes have been taking place slowly since the end of World War II. About 1953 the theaters lowered their color bar to admit all races. A few motels serve Negroes, and at times (during the Big League baseball training season) the hotels do likewise. CIO union activity has helped up-grade a few Negroes in some of the industries in Phoenix, and some stores have hired Negro clerks for the first time.[1]

One of the state's first interracial hospitals, and the first to offer nurse's training to women of every race and color, was erected in Phoenix shortly after the end of the war. The Urban League and the Greater Phoenix Council for Civic Unity were instrumental, about 1952, in stopping the segregation of Negro war veterans who had died; they brought about a change in the cemetery's policy so that all veterans could be buried together. The NAACP, the Anti-Defamation League, B'nai B'rith, as well as various church and other organizations, all worked to secure equal treatment for all racial and religious groups. Through the efforts of these groups as well as of articulate individuals, the discriminatory practices of drug stores, theaters, and restaurants are gradually being removed.

Attitudes between the minorities themselves are reported to be generally "good" although there is a tendency for the Spanish-Americans to look down on the Negroes. A few Spanish-American restaurants refuse service to Negroes; yet discrimination is the exception rather than the rule between the two groups.

More than two years after the permissive law was passed in 1951,[2] Phoenix announced plans for partial integration beginning in the fall of 1953. The Phoenix branch of the Arizona Teachers Association had gone on record in 1951 as favoring complete integration of all schools, and the high school administration also favored total integration. The school boards, however, felt that to move too quickly would

1. Cornell University Studies of Intergroup Relations, Social Science Research Center.
2. See Chapter 2, pp. 31-32.

upset race relations in the community. No effort was made to sample public opinion on this issue, but the school administrations accepted the board's decision on partial desegregation. The press, which had fought the mandatory bill, was now sympathetic to desegregation on a permissive local basis and published favorable editorials and news stories without complaints from its readers.

Phoenix elementary schools had operated on a segregated basis since about the time of World War I. In 1952 there were four elementary schools and one high school for Negroes only. These were located in three of the school districts. Negro children living in the other districts were transported to District 1 schools. District 1 is in the center of Phoenix but not contiguous with city boundaries. Some county districts paid transportation and tuition costs for Negro students to attend these schools, thus avoiding the issue of desegregation in their own districts.

The administration in District 1 was proud of the facilities it offered Negro children and felt that they were equal to the white schools. The Roosevelt district provided a good sized, modern school for Negroes, and there were no plans for desegregation in this district in 1953. Nor did District 7 plan integration although it was reputed to have some of the least desirable facilities in the state for its Negro children.

The three schools for Negroes in District 1 accommodated about one-fifth of the total enrollment for the district in 1953. There were 1,712 students and 60 teachers in the three schools. The high school for Negroes, Carver, had 450 students and a faculty of 20 at that time.

The high school board and some informed Negroes agreed that the facilities at the segregated high school were equal to those of the schools for whites. However, it was felt that the location, surrounded by warehouses and junk yards, was unfortunate. Athough Negroes could not attend the six union high schools, they had been permitted in the Phoenix Technical School and the Junior College. They could enroll in the regular summer school classes at Phoenix Union High, a prohibited school during the regular term. A Negro had taught classes in summer school without any objection from the community.

In the late spring of 1951, after the new state law had been passed, a committee approached the Phoenix Union High School Board with a request for desegregation. The committee was made up of representatives of the Greater Phoenix Council for Civic Unity, Anti-Defamation League, B'nai B'rith, NAACP, and the Social Action Committee of the First Presbyterian Church. The board said to this that the high school district voted in 1925 to authorize site purchase and construction of "a colored department of the Phoenix High School." The school board stated that it did not have the legal and moral right to desegregate the Carver School without an authorizing vote of the people.

After this declaration and upon the advice of various civic organizations, the local NAACP decided upon another approach. When the next term began, Negro children appeared at two schools for whites and asked to be registered there; school officials turned them away. The NAACP then brought suit against the school board in federal district court (*Phillips* v. *Phoenix Union High School District*). This case was turned over to the State Superior Court. The judge ruled that the language of the Arizona statute of 1951 authorizing local school boards to segregate groups of people was unconstitutional. The jurist declared that the effect of the statute was to transfer the responsibility for desegregation to local school authorities and held that such delegation was clearly unconstitutional. He emphasized that it was particularly true in this case in which the legislature had delegated its power to an administrative board without at the same time establishing a standard, criterion, or guide as to the circumstances under which such power might be exercised.

In this connection the judge cited an Arizona Supreme Court decision which found that "It is fundamental to our system of government that the rights of men are to be determined by laws and not by administrative officers or bureaus, and that this principle cannot be surrendered for convenience or nullified for the sake of expedience." The court thus held that the portion of the state law which provided that boards of trustees may "segregate groups of pupils" was unconstitutional and that a permanent injunction should be issued restraining the Phoenix Union High School from segregating students.

The school administration appealed to the State Supreme Court, and the appeal, of course, had the effect of staying the injunction against segregation. In the meantime and without an authorizing vote of the electorate in the high school district, the high school board decided on a move toward partial desegregation. Elementary School District 1, which included the greatest concentration of Negroes, also made some plans for desegregation.

For the fall term of 1953, high schools were rezoned, and students attended the school nearest their homes. Carver was retained as an "open" school without regard to zoning. Any student in the high school district could attend this school. The reasons advanced for retaining Carver were that otherwise the Negro teachers would be out of work (thus implying that there were no plans for the integration of teachers) and that Negro students would miss having their own band, orchestra, and other extra-curricular activities (implying that these activities might not be open on an integrated basis in the other schools). It was the opinion of the board that Negro students would elect to return to Carver when they met the stiffer competition in the integrated schools. Therefore the board announced that it would keep Carver open from two to five years even though some teachers might have empty class rooms. Some small towns near Phoenix formerly had sent their Negro students here, but they had integrated their schools, thus reducing Carver's enrollment anyway.

The elementary school board of District 1 began an integration program at the same time. It involved only kindergarten through third grade where children attended the school nearest their homes. Plans were to complete the integration program during the 1954-1955 school year.

The administrative decisions made at this time in Phoenix resemble those of Evansville, Indiana. It will be recalled that this city likewise kept its school for Negroes open while at the same time it allowed any student to elect either school in his district. However, the reactions of the Negro communities in these two towns were somewhat different. In Evansville the Negroes were slow to take advantage of the new arrangements. In Phoenix an active campaign was launched among Negro parents asking them not to send their children to the segregated schools. By the spring of 1954 Carver had only 350 students, a decrease of 100 in enrollment over the period of a year.

No plans were made in either of the districts to incorporate the Negro teachers in the system. Leaders of both racial groups expressed the opinion that Negro teachers would find it increasingly difficult to secure employment in the system even though they had tenure, unless faculties were integrated. The Negro teachers, under these circumstances, felt that the price of desegregation of the student populations might be too high. They reacted against the piecemeal arrangement somewhat as did the teachers in New Albany and Jeffersonville, Indiana. Without a clear and openly stated policy on teacher integration and tenure, tensions increased among the Negro staff. They did not know whether to push for desegregation, their obvious goal, or hold on to a school which had been carefully developed to be equal to the white schools.

In the meantime, the opinions of the high school board with regard to keeping Carver open had changed. At a board meeting in March, 1954, the following resolution was adopted unanimously:

1. that Carver High School shall continue to function as a unit of this system only through the remainder of the current school year, 1953-54;

2. that, thereafter, its faculty and, so far as is feasible, other employees shall be assigned to the other units of the System, at least two of its teachers to be assigned to each other existing unit, and

3. that, thereafter, its students shall be expected to attend the other schools of the System under rules applicable to all students who reside within the Phoenix Union High Schools and Phoenix College District...

4. that we declare our gratitude to the Negro community which for a quarter of a century has devoted itself to the success and support of this school but which now recognizes the closing of this school as symbolic of a great change not only in this community but in the nation at large....

The elimination of Carver School, and the increasing integration of Negro children in the elementary schools, will probably mean that Phoenix will have passed through the phase of segregated schools before some of the other communities in this study and before the Supreme Court of the United States issues instructions for the orderly process of desegregation for the states which still have segregated schools.

Where there is a complicated administrative structure such as in Phoenix, and where school administrators do not have the active support of their boards in making changes in the system, it is very difficult for civic and interracial organizations to furnish effective leadership. There is some evidence that the leadership in these groups had been discouraged over the complexity of the situation and, except for the school suit, had not made a consistent effort to interest all citizens in the issue. No evidence was ever produced to show that there would be resistance to desegregation should the schools decide on a total program.

The Smaller Arizona Communities

Turning to other Arizona communities, the most striking fact in both Douglas and Nogales was the money and effort these two small towns expended to keep a very few Negro students from going to school with Anglo- and Spanish-Americans.

Douglas: Douglas is unique in this survey in that it represents a completely segregated town so far as Negroes are concerned yet the policy of the school administration was directed consistently toward integration. It illustrates clearly that the respect given an able school administrator can be stronger than obvious prejudice and that integrated schools can function without disabling opposition in such an environment. The city of Douglas owes its existence to extensive mining activities in the surrounding area. It is also the trading center for a widely scattered rural population. The city had a population of 9,942 in 1950, of which about 62 per cent were Spanish-American, only about 1 per cent Negro, and the rest Anglo-American.

Spanish-Americans live primarily in the southern half of the city, in one suburban settlement. Aside from a few Negro families in one street, Negroes are not concentrated in any one area.

Negroes are discriminated against in practically all public accommodations. The city transportation system makes no distinction, but the Southern Pacific to Phoenix has a separate car for Negroes. Most of the restaurants will not serve them; Spanish-American eating places will prepare food for them to take out but will not serve them in the restaurant. There are two Negro-owned hotels and restaurants. Negroes are permitted in drive-in theaters, but only one regular movie house admits them and then only to the balcony. No drug store serves Negroes at the counter. Job opportunities are limited to manual work, with the exception of the two Negro teachers who are the only Negro persons in professional occupations in the town.

There is less discrimination against Spanish-Americans. They are free to patronize public establishments, and many are employed as clerks in such places. They also work in the smelter and other small industries in town. Their limitations in employment seem to be more a matter of skills and education than of discriminatory practices.

Douglas has a long history of segregation. With the growth of the town and the diffusion of power, changes have taken place gradually. Until after World War II, Spanish-American children were segregated, as were the Negro children.

The Douglas school system is organized on a 4-2-3-3 plan. There are six elementary, one intermediate, one junior, and one senior high school. Before desegregation one elementary school had only thirty-two Negro pupils and two teachers. Of the present school populations, three are predominantly Spanish-American, and two have almost equal proportions of the two groups. One school is primarily Anglo-American.

The first move toward desegregation was a rezoning action which distributed the Spanish-Americans throughout the schools. In 1947, because of the extremely crowded and inadequate facilities of the high school for Negroes, the superintendent secured permission from the board to transfer these students to an integrated high school. A similar argument in 1949 resulted in integration of the seventh through the ninth grades. When Arizona passed its permissive statute in 1951, the superintendent proposed complete integration. One board member objected, and for a year nothing was done. The superintendent felt that he should have the unanimous backing of the board to take such action. At the end of the year the member withdrew his objection and plans were made to complete the process.

The program went into effect in the fall of 1952. The pattern of Negro residences was such that there were Negro pupils in every school. There were, however, only thirty-two Negro children in grades one through six who until this time had been segregated.

The two Negro teachers were retained, one in the junior high school, the other as a first grade teacher. The superintendent did not plan to hire additional Negro staff.

The desegregation occurred without incident. A number of individuals objected at first, but no civic organization either supported or opposed it. The Negroes were in favor of it because of the less adequate facilities in the school formerly used by them, but they were not organized to support the action as a cause. Only the Teachers Association went on record favoring complete integration. School officials attributed the success of the program partly to the fact that it was treated as a *fait accompli,* leaving no room for argument.

Nogales: The 1950 census listed the population of Nogales as 6,153, with fewer than 100 Negro families. Approximately 70 per cent of the total population is Spanish-American. Much of the employment in the town is with the federal government since it is a border town and a gateway to Mexico.

The Negro people of Nogales are different in certain respects from those described elsewhere in these studies. They came to the area during World War I as soldiers in an Army camp. After the war, some settled here, inter-married with Spanish-Americans, and were accepted by this group. School segregation was the result of Anglo-American attitudes and practices, and it caused some unusual arrangements for the interracial families. In several families the non-Negro partner had children from a former marriage. In such families the Spanish-American children were required to attend the non-segregated school while those of mixed heritage went to the segregated school for Negroes. Discrimination in this town seems to be almost completely on the basis of color. Persons of lighter complexion are assumed to be Spanish-American and are not discriminated against, whereas the darker individuals are usually refused service in places of public accommodation.

Until thirty years ago, Spanish-American children were also in separate schools. This practice was stopped by the present superintendent shortly after he took office. Segregation of Negroes began just as soon as there were a few Negro children in the school system following World War I. However, the high school always operated on an integrated basis.

In the fall of 1952 Nogales desegregated its schools completely. The superintendent used as his argument the fact that it was needlessly expensive to maintain one school with two teachers for only twenty-three Negro students. Plans for integration were worked out carefully by the superintendent and the elementary supervisor before they were presented to the school board for approval. When the plans were announced to the teachers, there were no objections. The school administrators did, however, try to assign Negro pupils to classrooms where it was known that the teacher would be sympathetic. The two Negro teachers—and the janitor of the Negro school—were integrated into the system.

There were a few objections from parents, but most of the community supported the superintendent who had the confidence of the townsfolk through his long years of association with the school system.

Before school opened in the fall, the superintendent wrote

simple notes of welcome to the Negro children, telling them the name of their new school and teacher. Teachers were also given the names of their Negro pupils. No special indoctrination classes or meetings were held either for teachers, parents, or the children. In a community accustomed to differing ethnic groups, this change was not revolutionary.

Mount Holly, New Jersey

In spite of the fact that Mount Holly was *required* to desegregate its schools and Phoenix was *permitted* to, under their respective state laws, the parallels in the two communities are worth careful attention. Because of the resistance in Mount Holly, to the point at which the Division Against Discrimination thought that official action would have to be taken against the school administration, the discussion of this community is included in this chapter.

Mount Holly is in Burlington County, not far from the city of Burlington. It had a population of approximately 9,000 people in 1950, of whom almost 6 per cent were Negro. In Mount Holly, initial resistance to desegregation was manifested by the school board itself and by the man who was superintendent. By September, 1948, not only had no plans been made for desegregation, but for the first time the fifth and sixth grade Negro children were segregated in a separate building on the school grounds with one Negro teacher. At this point representatives of the DAD met with the board and secured an agreement that the first move in the desegregation process would be the reintegration of these students the following year. However, the teacher involved in the change was not assigned a regular class but was given the task of preparing a course of study for the fifth grade.

The board refused to desegregate or eliminate a two-room school in a Negro neighborhood on the grounds that it served its residential community and was not, therefore, segregated.

The DAD contested this and pointed out that the Negro children were forced to attend combined classes rather than graded ones as the white children did. The local Board of Education was called on to show cause why the commissioner of education should not withdraw state financial aid. So adamant was the board that the state officials were under the impression that Mount Holly intended to make a case to test the legality of the constitution in this respect. The children involved in this hot debate were sixty Negro youth in one elementary school.

During the summer of 1950 the parents of the Negro students laid plans for definite action at the beginning of the fall term. On opening day a small group of parents appeared at one of the schools for whites with their children and asked that the children be admitted to that school. Admission was denied, and the Negroes returned home in an orderly fashion. Meanwhile, no Negro children had appeared at the segregated school. The school administrators advised the board that the issue of segregation would have to be settled. However, the board refused to call an emergency meeting, saying that it would be considered at the regular meeting in a few days. Still no Negro children went to the school for Negroes.

At the meeting several days later, the board was faced with the necessity of ordering its attendance officer to carry out the compulsory attendance law of the state or of yielding to pressure from the parents and the State Board of Education. After a long session, the board yielded, and to show that it meant to change, it offered for sale the old segregated school building. It voted that the school be closed immediately and that the students be placed in the other schools. Since all teacher assignments had been made for the year, the two Negro teachers were given roving assignments as substitutes in all grades and also served as testing and writing specialists. The following year when vacancies occurred, they were assigned to regular grades.

Predictions of community resentment did not materialize. There were less than half a dozen protests from white parents and no organized opposition at all. Before integration there had been two PTA's, one for each race. The organization now is on a school basis, and the Negro parents participate in about the same proportion as do the whites.

No special preparation or instructions were given either teachers or students, nor were any unpleasant incidents reported. One Negro teacher was assigned to a class in which there were no Negro students, without protest from parents. The school administrators reported that in the past there had sometimes been incidents involving Negro children who were entering an integrated situation for the first time but that since the whole system was integrated, no such incidents had occurred.

It is the policy of the administration to avoid placing only one Negro child in a class, and the other extreme of seeking an even balance of races has also been avoided. There is still some concern among high school administrators because the Negro youth tend to cluster together in the cafeteria. It was suggested that in regard to integrated recreational activities there was a lack of effective leadership in the Negro community.

The vital role played by the school board in the initial stages of planning for desegregation is clearly illustrated in the case of Phoenix, Douglas, and Mount Holly. In such small, responsible groups the conservative opinions held by some members, or the fears of the members that the community will not support "radical" changes, can delay any move for some time. However, it seems equally obvious that the leavening influence of progressive but not radical members may, over a period of time, convince a board that a community will support measures not formerly thought possible. In neither Phoenix nor Mount Holly was information available to show what specific event or argument turned the tide, but when the change was made, it was complete. Where Mount Holly offered the old school building for sale, Phoenix made plans either to dispose of the former high school for Negroes or put it to non-classroom use, probably as a warehouse for the school system.

The about-face of these two school administrations can not be taken to mean a complete change of heart on the part of those who had objected to integration. More likely, they have seen that half-way measures in desegregation may appear to some parents as unfair to those children who attend segregated schools while others are in an integrated situation. In this respect, in none of the communities studied does the piecemeal approach appear to have worked as harmoniously as a complete change under a careful plan of action.

CHAPTER 9

Patterns of Adjustment:

CARLSBAD, LAS CRUCES, ALAMOGORDO AND
ROSWELL, NEW MEXICO *

THE ONLY COMMUNITIES IN NEW MEXICO WHICH HAVE EVER
taken the option offered by the permissive nature of the
state law to maintain segregated schools have been located
in the southeastern section of the state, near Texas and the
Mexican border. The area has sometimes been called "little
Texas," partly in recognition of the prevalence here of
"Southern" attitudes and patterns of behavior in race relations. The six communities included in this survey illustrate
the variations within this segregated pattern and the different methods employed in the initial desegregation process. Each of the communities has a distinctly individual
character, each is dependent on a different base for its economic life, and each has a different proportional representation of the three ethnic groups most common to the area. Four
of these towns—Carlsbad, Las Cruces, Alamagordo, and Roswell—took steps to desegregate the schools before the Supreme Court decision; these will be discussed in this chapter.
Two—Hobbs and Clovis—made no overt move in this direction until after May 17, 1954. Because the situations faced
by the school administrations were somewhat different in

* Based on the report of field research prepared by Margaret W. Ryan,
Cornell University.

these towns, they will be treated in the following chapter.

All public schools in New Mexico are supported primarily by the State Maintenance Fund, distributed on the basis of need to each county. Local funds complete the school budgets. Within the communities studied, the state funds varied from 70 to about 90 per cent of the total school budget. Teachers are paid on a uniform state salary scale, one of the highest in the nation. If a teacher has completed three years of sastisfactory work in a system and is given a contract for the fourth year, his tenure is then assured in the system by state law. This tenure law is now under some criticism since it has implications for the status of Negro teachers in the systems which are now desegregating.

All municipal school systems operate with a five-member board of education, elected for staggered terms. Some, like Hobbs, also have an advisory committee which is appointed by the board. The superintendent of schools is appointed by the Board of Education.

Carlsbad

Carlsbad is one of the older towns in this section of New Mexico, and its established character is evident from the type of residential neighborhoods and from the appearance of its business district. It is heavily dependent on potash mining as well as on the tourist trade from those who come to look at the famous caverns near by. Although it has grown in the past decade, this growth has been at a slower pace than in some of the neighboring towns, and the new residents have been absorbed into the life of the community with little change in the usual patterns of community life.

Informed persons in Carlsbad said that most of the residents traced their ancestry to Southern states, particularly Texas and Oklahoma. Members of the Spanish-American community claimed that this regional origin was responsible for the segregation and discrimination found in the town. By 1954 the population was estimated at 26,000, of whom about 70 per cent were thought to be Anglo-Americans, 25 per cent Spanish-Americans, and 5 per cent Negroes. Most of the Spanish-Americans were fairly recent immigrants from Mexico and were not part of the older, more established Latin culture of the state.

The Negro dwellings were concentrated in the southern part of the town. Most were south of the canal, a traditional boundary line, although some lived in a neighborhood adjacent to a white elementary school north of the canal. This small settlement of Negro families became an important part of the desegregation picture in Carlsbad. Spanish-Americans were not confined to any one neighborhood, but they tended to concentrate in the same residential areas with the Negroes. The Negro area also housed a number of white families in a veterans' housing project. This area was uneven in appearance, some of the homes approximating those to be expected in a slum area, but others neat and well cared for, constructed of cinder block, plastered, with green lawns and carefully tended shrubbery. A stranger could not have distinguished between the homes of Anglo-Americans, Spanish-Americans, or Negroes in many instances in this particular area of town.

Carlsbad is a "strong union town," both because of the mines and of the construction industry. Neither industry used Negroes in any capacity other than as unskilled labor. Except for the school teachers and a few ministers, there were no professionally employed Negroes in the town, and very few Negroes held jobs which could be called skilled. There were no Negroes employed by the city and only one Spanish-American who was a deputy-sheriff.

Public facilities were open to Spanish-Americans with no discrimination but most were prohibited for the Negroes. Some hotels, motels, and restaurants would serve Negroes if they were accompanied by white patrons or were members of sports teams, but the usual pattern was to refuse service or to serve individual Negroes in cars at the drive-in restaurants. There was no swimming pool, the river being the usual place for aquatic sports. By custom the Negroes used the east side of the river, the rest of the community the west. Within the past two years the city's playgrounds and the summer recreational program had been integrated, and service clubs had sponsored Little League baseball teams. These programs were given credit for improved attitudes among the three ethnic groups. All ethnic groups could attend any movie house and sit in any section of the audience.

There were no strong intergroup agencies in Carlsbad. As in all towns in New Mexico, with the exception of Albuquerque, there was neither a YWCA nor a YMCA. A small chapter of the NAACP was not very active, nor was the Anti-Defamation League.

It was the opinion of informed members of the community that there was considerable prejudice on the part of the Anglo-Americans toward both the Spanish-Americans and the Negroes, but that this prejudice was diffuse and more apparent in the lack of communication between the groups than in any overt tension between them. The few Spanish-American families who were members of the middle and upper socioeconomic class had little or nothing to do with the poorer and more recent immigrants from Mexico. In the neighborhood in which all three groups lived, relations were said to be good.

There were nine elementary schools in the Carlsbad system, and two additional schools were due to open in the fall of 1954, one of them located within a few blocks of the Carver School. Carver was the elementary school to which all Negro children went, regardless of their residential district in the town. Two junior high schools, one in the southern and one in the northern section of the town, and a centrally located high school completed the system. None of the buildings, except the two under construction, were built recently, but all appeared to have sufficient playground space, and most were well kept in appearance. The senior high school was also used as the Carlsbad Instructional Center, a branch of the New Mexico Agricultural and Mechanical College.

Until 1951 the Negroes had attended Carver School through all grades. As early as 1948 the superintendent began discussions with his board, suggesting that the high school students from Carver should be allowed to go to Carlsbad High, where they would have a wider choice in courses. He told the board that he would take the responsibility for the suggestion. The board agreed to the change on the basis of the monetary savings to the system since the high school classes at Carver were very small. With board agreement, the superintendent then talked individually with every faculty member and with all the principals, taking an informal and confidential poll of opinion in this group. Most did not object to the idea of desegregation at this level. Discussions with community leaders usually brought forth the comment that times were changing, the Korean War had hastened the change, and that "we might as well go along with it since we can't stop it." The Ministerial Alliance had been cooperative. Individual members preached sermons on the subject of brotherhood in the various churches; but the advice from this group, as well as from community leaders was, "Go slow; don't push too fast."

In the spring of 1951 the superintendent talked with the senior high school graduating class, asking them to consider letting the one senior at Carver come to Carlsbad High to participate in the graduation exercises with that class. The Spanish-American boy who was president of the class suggested that the students conduct a survey of opinion in the group. As a result, the class voted for integration at the high school level, the Negro boy appeared to graduate with this class, and the following year the Negro high school students at Carver were moved to Carlsbad High. A year later the junior high school was desegregated, leaving Carver as an elementary school only.

Until that time Carver had had only Negro students, but at the time the secondary school was desegregated, some Spanish-American pupils were assigned to this school, making it bi-racial in composition, although no Anglo-American children went there. It was the intention of the superintendent to move children from other groups to Carver rather than to try to integrate the Negro children into the other elementary schools in the system. He and the board felt that this would be more acceptable to the majority of the residents of Carlsbad. It was said that the superintendent received only one objection from a parent during this entire process, and that was, "Our only objection is that you have done this in such a way that we can't complain."

When the high school was desegregated in 1951, those Negro teachers without tenure were not re-employed, and several Anglo- and Spanish-American teachers were placed at Carver. While there is no stated policy with regard to hiring Negro teachers, it was the feeling among informed persons that as Negroes resigned, they would be replaced with Anglo- or Spanish-American teachers.

School district lines are used for all schools except Carver. Some Negro children who live in the adjoining district, just north of the canal and very close to another elementary school, are transported by bus to the Carver School. White children within walking distance of Carver are transported about five miles into the country to a school for only white children. Residents in the Carver district said they were waiting to see what the district line would be and what the school administration policy would be with regard to the new elementary school which was being constructed within walking distance of Carver. The school is to open in the fall of 1954, but no announcement had been made of the district it was to serve.

However, the NAACP announced in the summer of 1954 that it intended to file suit on behalf of the elementary children who were transported by bus to the Carver School, on the grounds that this practice continued to segregate Negro children in the elementary grades, in spite of the fact that Spanish-American children also attended Carver School. No action had been taken in this matter at the time of this study.

The Carlsbad school system had recently inaugurated a program of teaching Spanish to all Anglo-American and Negro children, starting in the first grade. The program was to be extended each year to each grade following, until Spanish would be taught in all grades. At the sixth grade, Spanish-American children were to join the classes. This program was designed to improve the understanding of the place of Spanish culture in the Southwest. However, lack of interest and attention among the Negro children at Carver caused the program to be discontinued temporarily in that school. Until the mid-1920's, all Spanish-American children had attended a segregated school; the first move to eliminate this pattern also occurred at the high school level. By 1954 there were Spanish-Americans in all the schools although residential concentration tended to keep the proportion higher in some elementary schools than in others.

The desegregation process in Carlsbad was considered successful by all informants, including the members of the Negro community, in spite of the fact that Carver was not districted for Negro pupils. The only difficulties encountered had been when bi-racial teams from the schools had played in neighboring towns which had not yet desegregated their schools. The administration makes it a policy not to keep records by race, but it was estimated that there were approximately twenty Negro youth in each of the junior high schools and about half that number in the high school. The Carlsbad Instructional Center has been integrated since its inception in 1950.

By the fall of 1954 there were only three Negro teachers and the Negro principal in the system, and it seemed evident that teaching as a career for Negroes in Carlsbad would be very limited for some years to come. However, faculty meetings, both formal and social, were integrated, as were other professional groups and committees.

Las Cruces

The town of Las Cruces is situated in the midst of a rich, agricultural plain north of El Paso, Texas. The irrigated lands furnish one of the major sources of income for the town which until recently was only a trading center for the region. To the south of Las Cruces a few miles is the New Mexico Agricultural and Mechanical College, one of the largest educational institutions in the state. To the east rises a range of sawtoothed mountains, dominating the fertile fields below.

The Spanish influence in Las Cruces is evident in the narrow streets through much of the business section and the older residential areas, in the prevalence of adobe homes and buildings, many of them flush with the sidewalk or the street. One sees as many Spanish-Americans as Anglo-Americans and hears as much Spanish as English spoken on the streets and in the shops.

The population of Dona Ana county is estimated at 25,000, of whom about 6,000 are Anglo-Americans recently arrived to work at the White Sands Proving Ground north of Las Cruces. The town itself has about 16,500 inhabitants, of whom slightly more than half are Anglo-American, slightly less than half Spanish-American, and about 2 per cent are Negro. The area to the northeast of the town center, with its dusty roads and small box-like adobe houses, is home to the Negro community and to many Spanish-Americans in the lower economic levels. A few Anglo-American families also live in this area. However, there are Spanish-American families in all socioeconomic levels and in all residential neighborhoods in Las Cruces, and they are accepted in all social and civic activities and groups. One Spanish-American informant said that up until fifteen or twenty years ago the Spanish kept to themselves and did not associate with Anglo-Americans but that at present there was much more informal association between the two groups at all social levels. He considered this to be to the advantage of both groups. A number of informants also said that the Negro community was old and settled, that the families were respected and accepted in the civic life of the community. However, it was indicated that they usually kept to themselves for their informal associations, except in the case of immediate neighbors in the bi-racial area.

Other than the Negro school teachers, of whom there were four in 1954, and the Negro ministers, there were no other professionally employed Negroes, and there were very few in the skilled trades. Most were employed in unskilled labor, even those whose education would have fitted them for better jobs. One informant said that one young man, a graduate of New Mexico Agricultural and Mechanical College in journalism, was employed as a dishwasher in a local restaurant.

There were no limitations on employment for Spanish-Americans. The mayor and two of the city councilmen were from this group, and a number held other positions in the city government. There were representatives in all the professions as well as in the skilled trades.

Although Las Cruces is smaller than Hobbs or Carlsbad, and the trading center for an agricultural area, the attitudes and practices with regard to discrimination were less strict. Negroes had been accepted as guests in hotels and motels, and most restaurants and drug stores would serve them in spite of the ever present sign reserving the right to refuse service to anyone. The city swimming pool, opened in 1950, had always been integrated and so were the movies. As one informant said, "Las Cruces is more cosmopolitan than most towns in southeastern New Mexico."

One of the most active agencies in human relations has been the Ministerial Alliance which makes a practice of including a Negro minister in its Good Friday and Easter services. The United Council of Church Women is bi-racial. A chapter of NAACP with about seventy members had been conducting a membership drive but had not been engaged in a particularly active program recently.

In spite of the generally tolerant attitude of its citizens, the schools in Las Cruces remained segregated until the fall of 1953 when the junior and senior high schools were combined at the schools which were formerly for whites. The first classes included about twenty-two Negro youth in these schools. The Negro elementary pupils remained at Washington School in a segregated situation even though the district included both Anglo- and Spanish-American families. Washington School was one of the least well equipped schools in the system.

The Las Cruces system was consolidated in the spring of 1954. The system then included eight elementary schools, one junior and one senior high school, with about 5,000 students. One of the elementary schools was new and was to be in operation for the first time in the fall of 1954. Most of the Spanish-American children attended one of the elementary schools whether or not they lived in its district. This seemed to be more a matter of parental choice than of a stated policy on the part of the school administration. Schools have not been strictly districted, and it was said that there was considerable movement of pupils from one school to another. In some instances this was the result of school bus routes, the school lunch program or personal choice where the schools were known to have exceptionally good teachers. One board member said that because of the growth of the town, the board would have to consider strict districting in the near future in order to assure equitable distribution of pupils among the available facilities.

When the Negro students went to the one high school for the first time, it was the opinion of both the Negro and the white community that the Negro boys would have an easier time adjusting to the new situation than would the girls, because they had participated in bi-racial sports meets in the past. One high school teacher, who admitted that she had thought the Negroes would have a hard time, said that everyone in the school administration was surprised at how well the Negro students fitted in. The junior class elected a Negro boy as president within a few weeks of the opening of school. It was the opinion of the school officials that the class had done this to make the Negroes feel at home, for they had not known the boy except as an athlete. However, he was well liked by his classmates. A reiterated statement was that if the parents would just stay out of it, the students would get along very well together.

A guidance officer said that there had been no incidents between the Negroes and the white students and that on the whole the Negro students had kept up a good average in their studies. Only one in the junior and one in the senior high school had dropped out, and one of these had a long record of scholastic difficulty in Washington School. One school official said, however, that dating between Anglo-Americans and Spanish-Americans was becoming more usual and that some parents objected rather strongly to this practice.

When the junior and senior high schools were desegregated, those Negro teachers without tenure were dismissed, and the one teacher with tenure who had been in the system since 1943 was also dismissed. This teacher contested the decision of the administration, and her case was still pending in the State Supreme Court although she had won it at each level below there. According to her legal adviser, the superintendent had stated at the hearings that she was morally fit, loyal to the administration, and capable of teaching subjects for which she had been trained at the high school level. She was the wife of a prominent minister and very active in civic affairs in Las Cruces.

This teacher had indicated her willingness to accept another position in the school system if she did not have to sacrifice her tenure through doing so. She was offered a position in the cafeteria at approximately two-thirds of her former salary, provided she would resign and relinquish her seniority position on the teaching staff. This she refused to do. Her case is considered a test of the teacher tenure law in the state.

Informants in the Negro community said that because the case was well known, it was likely that the principal and the remaining Negro teachers of the Washington Elementary School would be reluctant to push for its desegregation until the results of the case were known. However, it was also said that under a new superintendent and a new school board, some persons felt that the policy would change so that within a year or so it would be possible to desegregate Washington without causing any community tension. The fact of the Supreme Court ruling made the situation in Las Cruces, with regard to the Negro teachers, more amenable to solution than similar situations in other communities described in previous chapters, which had arisen several years before the ruling.

As in Carlsbad, informants felt that the Anglo-American schools had received preferential treatment with regard to facilities and equipment, that the schools with predominantly Spanish-American students were next on the list, and that the school for Negroes was at the bottom. In Las Cruces the

Washington School had four classrooms, an auditorium which had been used for two classrooms at times, and a separate building for shop and home economics. Even in 1954 there was more than one class to a room, and some of the teachers were teaching subjects for which they had not been trained, said one Negro school official. It was a frequently expressed opinion of informed persons in the community that the resistance to desegregated schools had stemmed largely from the former superintendent and the school board and that the community as a whole had no objection to integrated schools. The action of the junior class was cited as illustrative of friendly feelings between the ethnic groups in the town. However, one influential Negro in the community said, "Let the wood burn to coal, let the coal turn to charcoal, the charcoal cool to ash; then the groups in Las Cruces can get along together without stirring up trouble."

Alamogordo

Alamogordo lies in a desert area just north of the White Sands Proving Ground and west of a range of semi-arid mountains. As late as 1947 it was a small town of approximately 3,500 people who depended on ranching, a lumber mill, and a railroad tie factory for their livelihood. With the reopening of an air base south of the town, it began to grow rapidly, including expansion of home building to accommodate the permanent personnel at the base. The population is now estimated at approximately 12,000 persons, of whom about two-thirds are Anglo-Americans, some 30 per cent Spanish-Americans, and 3 per cent Negroes.

Before the rapid spurt in growth, there had been as many Spanish-Americans as Anglo-Americans in town, and the Spanish-American children had been segregated in school. Because it was a relatively poor community, the Spanish-

Americans were for the most part laborers who were still very close to their original home in Mexico in habits and in their social values. The Negroes had come to work on the railroad or in the railroad shops which had formerly been in the town. The present Negro population is, for the most part, well established in the community.

One street, running east to west, had marked the dividing line between the Anglo-American and the Spanish-American parts of town. The Spanish-Americans lived in the southern half, along with a small Negro population, and the Anglo-Americans in the northern half. Apparently this segregation was "voluntary" with each group, in that the Spanish culture and the culture of the Anglo-Americans had little in common in this community. Most of the Anglo-Americans were southern in origin and held to their traditional attitudes toward other races and ethnic groups. Language, church, and family ties held the Spanish-Americans in a separate group.

Remnants of this division are present in Alamogordo today, though the sharp demarcation of sections of town has disappeared with the sudden influx of people from all sections of the United States. The Spanish-Americans are still inclined to keep to themselves; the division between Anglo- and Spanish-American peoples within the schools is fully known to the school administration which, however, is in some ways powerless to combat it.

Segregation has broken down to the extent that the Spanish-Americans are free to go anywhere or make use of any of the public facilities available, and there are both elected and appointed officials in the city government who belong to this group. A federal housing project on the south side of the residential area is completely integrated so far as racial composition is concerned, and a veterans' project on the northern fringe of town has some Spanish-American home owners. The Spanish-Americans are represented on all major city commissions, on the school board, and in all civic activities.

The pattern of segregation for the Negroes has changed more slowly. Hotels and motels will accept sports teams with bi-racial personnel, but apparently these are the only occasions on which Negroes have tried to get accommodations in town. Even though the restaurants do not, as a rule, display the sign reserving the right to refuse service, Negroes usually do not try to be served in them. The city has a swimming pool which is segregated in the sense that there is a special day set aside for the use of the Negroes. The movies make no distinction, but other recreational activities on a commercial basis are still segregated.

Indicative of the transitional pattern is the fact that most Little League baseball teams are bi-racial. However, the sponsor of one team made sure that the Negro lad on one team did not appear more than once, although he was considered to be one of the best players.

The present superintendent has been in the system since 1947. His first move in office was to see that the division between Spanish-American and Anglo-American schools was eliminated. Community leaders credited him with reducing the social significance of the formerly sharp line which divided the town.

However, even after the Spanish-American children were distributed among the various elementary schools, a segregated school for Negroes remained—one with no more than two or three teachers each year for the entire twelve grades. Because the graduates from this school did not have the educational qualifications required of high school graduates by the state, the local school system was criticized by the State Board of Education.

Even before 1947, the local school board had come to believe that something had to be done to equalize the standards of the school for Negroes, and because of the small enrollment, it seemed evident that equalization would mean desegregation. In 1951 the high school students from the segregated school were moved into the Alamogordo High School, and apparently they were incorporated into the school activities without protests from the Anglo-American community. In support of this statement, several informants cited the outstanding Negro athletes of the past few years.

Two years later the elementary students from the school for Negroes were transferred to the other elementary schools, and the former segregated school was retired as a classroom building. There were only about fifty Negro students in the entire school. At this time the Negro teacher with tenure was placed in the high school. Another testimony to the changing community attitudes was that he was one of the most popular teachers in the school. Although he could counsel only about thirty students, over 200 requested him as their counselor. Every informant deplored his untimely death and mentioned the fact that the high school annual that year was dedicated to him. One school official hazarded the guess that there would be no objection to hiring another Negro teacher as this teacher had dispelled the myth that a Negro could not teach white children.

The segregation problems faced by the Alamogordo school administration arose in part from some elements in the Spanish-American community. Experience in this town was different from that encountered in any other included in the study. Because the Latin population was still very close to its origins in Mexico, and thus in a sociological sense marginal in a new culture, there was fertile ground for the development of divergent groups. Two of these were the Blue Cross, a secret Spanish-American organization, and the Pachucos, an ideological brother of the zoot-suiters. Both flourished for a short time in Alamogordo among high school youth and the youth recently out of school.

Members of the Blue Cross could be recognized by a tattoo between thumb and forefinger, and, if the individual were an officer, a further tattoo near the knuckles of the hand. Apparently the purpose of the organization was to see that no privilege was granted to any other group that was not also shared equally by the Blue Cross members. A school official said, however, that they were unwilling to share equally in the responsibilities of citizenship. The Pachucos, whose membership overlapped that of the Blue Cross, were recognizable by their distinctive costume—wooden-soled shoes with taps, trousers low on the hips, peg pants. Both groups exhibited characteristics of "marginal" groups. In the fall of 1953 the high school administration felt that their influence was detrimental to the morale of the entire student body, and a concerted effort was made to discourage their activity. By Christmas, two members had been convicted and sentenced to the penitentiary for bringing "wet-backs" into the United States, and a high school youth had been sent to the state reformatory for breaking and entering a building. Although it was not proved, many people thought that these groups were actively involved in smuggling wet-backs into the country and in the distribution of marijuana. The active participation of the high school administration in the presentation of evidence against members of both groups did much to eliminate their influence in the community.

One informant thought that the activities of these two groups might reflect the desire on the part of the Spanish-Americans to establish a parochial school in Alamogordo. The self-imposed segregation of this group was indicated by the fact that seniors of Spanish-American descent did not take part in the baccalaureate exercises of the graduating class.

On the other hand, some evidence of ethnic cooperation was found in the operation of the PTA's. There were three PTA branches, one for all elementary schools, one for the secondary schools, and one for the air base. Participation in the PTA's appeared to be as great for the two minority groups as for the Anglo-Americans. The G.I. Forum was also organized without regard to race or color and was very active in civic affairs. The USO was open to all servicemen and a favorite spot for them in town. The Spanish-Americans who participated in the forum and in the USO activities were those who were well assimilated into American culture.

Experience in Alamogordo illustrates the problems facing a school administration when there is voluntary segregation of a minority group. It points to the fact that the schools can be a positive force in intergroup relations in a community which has grown too rapidly to assimiliate all its new citizens easily. Alamogordo had changed from a small hamlet into a busy and growing young town, and the growing pains were still in evidence in 1954.

Roswell

Roswell lies in the middle of a fertile irrigated plain and derives its wealth and stability from irrigated farms, live-stock, some tourist trade, and the proximity of an Air Force base and the New Mexico Military Institute. Between 1940 and 1950 the population increased 90 per cent, and it is now estimated at approximately 30,500, of whom over three-fourths are Anglo-American, only about 3,500 are Spanish-American, and less than 1,000 are Negro. The Negro popula-tion tends to be relatively stable, having increased less, pro-portionately, than the other two groups. Some of the increase in Negro population can be attributed to air force personnel living off the base.

Informed citizens in the community said that Roswell was typical, in its attitudes toward minority groups, of towns further to the east which are considered to be Southern. Many of the "old timers" came from neighboring states in the South. More recent immigrants represent all regions of the United States, and this increasingly cosmopolitan composition is sometimes credited with a gradual change in patterns of discrimination within the community.

Spanish-Americans live in the southeastern quadrant of the city, but their neighborhoods also house some Negroes and Anglo-Americans. Most Negroes live south of the main east-west street, but there are no solidly Negro settlements. Their homes are found also north of this thoroughfare in predominantly Anglo-American neighborhoods. There are upper middle-class neighborhoods which have restrictive covenants although one informant said that it would be possible for some Negroes to purchase homes in certain of these areas.

At times there have been Spanish-Americans in elected or appointed positions in the city and county government, but there never have been any Negroes in such positions. There seems to be very little discrimination against Spanish-Americans in the matter of private employment. This is not true for the Negroes who are concentrated in the unskilled jobs, with the exception of a few Negro teachers and the Negro ministers.

Public facilities were open to Spanish-Americans, limited only by their ability to pay for the services or their interest in using them. For the Negro community the pattern, which had been completely segregated until World War II, was changing slowly. Some hotels, motels, and restaurants would serve athletic teams with bi-racial personnel, if prior arrangements were made. The hospital was open to all individuals on a non-segregated basis, and most doctors would take Negro patients.

However, some remnants of segregation remained in the city-sponsored recreation programs. There were three recreation centers, one for each group, located in the area of highest concentration of each. The swimming pool was limited to Anglo-Americans and Spanish-Americans, and plans were being discussed for the building of a pool in the area near the elementary school for Negroes.

Until a few years ago, there was one movie house which did not discriminate against Negroes, but as the result of one unpleasant incident, this theater refused further Negro patronage. Another movie reserved a section of the balcony for Negroes. The drive-ins made no distinction. Interestingly enough, since the integration of the junior and senior high schools, student activity tickets which include admission to movies at student rates have been accepted by all movie houses from Negro as well as other students.

The first school for Negroes was opened in Roswell in 1904 with one teacher. Until 1926 it was housed in rented quarters; about that time a two-room structure was built and another teacher employed. In 1937 a third room was added, but it was not until about 1950 that Carver was re-modeled and enlarged to its present capacity of five rooms. In 1953 it functioned with seven teachers in five rooms and included the first six years of schooling. All rooms house more than one class, and several grades attend only half-day sessions because of inadequate space. However, this split session arrangement is shared by other grades in the public schools, because the building program has not yet caught up with the rapid increase in enrollment.

Any improvement in Carver School was a direct result of interest the Negro students displayed in having a better school. As an illustration, it was said that about 1946 the Negro students told the principal that they were going on strike for better facilities. They remained out of school one day, parading with their banners through the business district and around all the white schools. Some public interest was aroused by this demonstration, but it was several years before any improvements were made. Then Negro leaders urged their people to vote for a school bond issue, on the grounds that without it nothing could be done to *any* school.

The issue passed, and the newspapers at that time stated that 60 per cent of the 211 votes cast were by Negroes. Shortly thereafter, Carver was enlarged.

The school administration had discussed the problem of the Negro junior and senior high school students who were not getting a full course of instruction because there was only one teacher for all subjects in these grades. Graduates had found that it was necessary to make up subjects such as language or science before they would be admitted to a college. Because of the small number of students involved, and the prohibitive cost of furnishing them equal but separate instruction, they were moved into the other junior and senior high schools in the fall of 1952. This initial group comprised about thirty students from the seventh through the twelfth grades. One school administrator said that there was no protest from Anglo-American parents because the number was so small that it made no visible difference in the composition of the school.

Informed persons in the Negro community said that those students who entered the high school had an easier time adjusting than did those who went to the junior high school. This statement was based on the policy of the high school administration of assigning Negro students only to those classes conducted by teachers known to be unprejudiced and helpful in the adjustments facing the Negro students. At the junior high school, this selection of teachers was not made, and some of the Negro youth felt that they were resented in the school. During the spring before the move was made, the administration had held conferences and meetings with the students at the junior and senior high school, preparing them for the change, and the teachers at Carver had their students enact in advance possible situations they might encounter in the desegregated schools to prepare them for handling effectively any contingency.

Several Negro students in the high school reported to the

Negro principal at Carver, "We'd like it better if the white kids wouldn't over-do it being nice to us, then we could all be natural." It was also reported that one Negro youth who had been a problem at Carver for a number of years, immediately sought out and was accepted by similar problem youth at the senior high school. Laughing, the informant said, "That, too, is integration!"

The relatively easy assimilation of the Negro youths was helped by the fact that Carver had a very active sports program, particularly in basketball. Carver had no gym and very little equipment on its playing field until about 1948 when the Negro community contributed the equipment for basketball. After some initial skirmishes with administrative personnel of the white school, the Carver youth were allowed to practice in the high school gym, where the boys made the acquaintance of some of the Anglo-American players. The Little League baseball teams, which are integrated, have also fostered friendly intergroup relations among those students who still remain in a segregated school.

School officials estimated that if Carver were either integrated or abandoned as a school building, there would be Negro pupils in five or six of the elementary schools. The proportion of Negro to other students in the elementary schools was about one in fifty. It was not felt that this would cause difficulty in the community. The problem, according to school officials, was what to do with the Negro teachers who had tenure. Of the seven Negro teachers, including the teaching principal, four had tenure, as they had been in the Roswell system from six to thirteen years. Of these, one was retired on physical disability, and it is doubtful that she will return to teaching. The three teachers without tenure will be eligible for that status, if their contracts are renewed for the 1955-56 school years.

By the time the Supreme Court announced its decision, school appointments and plans for the 1954-55 school year had been made. No formal discussions of the position of Carver under the new ruling came up at a school board meeting, but it was generally understood that the school would continue to operate as it had in the past until such time as the Court ruled on the process to be followed in total desegregation. All elementary schools in the system are districted with the exception of this one.

One school official remarked that the teachers with tenure were as good on the average as any in the school system. He said that they were responsible people who would probably see that Roswell was not ready for faculty integration and would resign. Two were married and had husbands with good jobs and the principal had a wife who worked. There seemed to be a lack of understanding that these teachers might not wish to give up their professional careers or that they might take pride in the accomplishments of the Negroes who had done well in the integrated system, even though they came in effect from the "little red school house."

The Negro teachers were well aware of the case pending in the State Supreme Court over the firing of a teacher with tenure in Las Cruces, and they knew that the final decision in that case, testing the constitutionality of the tenure law, would have direct bearing on their position in the Roswell system in a year or so. Apparently none of them contemplated resigning should Carver's students be desegregated, as the white official thought they would. One remarked that if the Supreme Court cases had been on the basis of teacher integration rather than student desegregation, both issues would have been settled at once since it would have been impossible for students to be segregated if the staff were not. He felt that the issue had become two-pronged and that this made it more difficult to settle.

Indicative of the basic attitudes of the community was the phrase used repeatedly by influential Anglo-American citizens, "Now, I don't feel about the darkies like some other people here do but...." Most Anglo-Americans attributed any race tension to the presence of Negroes from New York or California at the air force base although no one could recall any specific incident which might have led to overt trouble. It was the opinion of the Anglo-American informants that the indigenous Negro population "knew its place" and was satisfied with it. Negroes, on the other hand, said that they had been working steadily but not hastily to better the position of the group in the community and that it was not from the outside that the movement gained its support or strength.

There is a recently formed branch of the NAACP which had not been very active up to the summer of 1954, and it was not considered by the Negroes to furnish the leadership in the community. Should the problem of Negro teacher tenure arise, this situation might change.

Some members of the Negro community felt that the atmosphere of Roswell was becoming less discriminatory as the "old timers" retired and their positions of community leadership were assumed by a younger and more varied group. It was on the basis of such a change in the composition of the school board that they were not unduly worried about their positions should all schools be desegregated.

In three of these communities—Carlsbad, Las Cruces, and Roswell—community sentiments did not seem to be strongly opposed to total desegregation of the schools. Yet in each the elementary school has remained either totally segregated or the only one to which Negro pupils in those grades could go. The policy of the school boards seemed based on the assumption that were these schools abandoned and the Negro teachers assigned to the other schools in the systems, the community would react against it. It was impossible to ascertain whether this attitude reflected the position of the majority of the residents or if it was that of the boards themselves. In Alamogordo, where one Negro teacher had been assigned to a desegregated school, there was no unfavorable community comment. It is entirely possible that the combination of the State Teacher Tenure Law and the Supreme Court decision will result in total desegregation of these schools and in integration of faculties within a short period. Because of the small number of children involved in each town, and the smaller number in each school, it is unlikely that Anglo-Americans generally would react strongly against such a move.

CHAPTER 10

Response to the Supreme Court Decision:
HOBBS AND CLOVIS, NEW MEXICO *

THESE TWO TOWNS ARE SITUATED VERY CLOSE TO THE TEXAS border, Hobbs to the south, Clovis to the south-central border of New Mexico. Both are trading centers for many of the ranches of west Texas, and Clovis has even been the school center for children from near-by rural areas of Texas.

The school administrations in both towns had discussed the problem of desegregating the public schools, as much because of the expense of maintaining accredited junior and senior high schools for a very small number of Negro students, as because of the possible implications of the cases before the Supreme Court. However, administrators and school boards were hesitant to make the move because they felt that community sentiment would oppose it strongly. One school official said that his administration had hoped that the cases would not be decided until his town had completed its expansion program and was ready to face the issue.

The consensus among school officials seemed to be that the decision came too suddenly, without sufficient preparation at the local level, and that it would be difficult for the schools to justify their actions except as compliance with national laws. Several administrators expressed the opinion

* Based on the report of field research prepared by Margaret W. Ryan.

that the time lag between the first announcement from the Court and the final meeting to announce the possible methods to be employed had put them on the spot. If they did not comply now they would be subject to suit, and if they did comply, they would be subject to severe censure from local residents. Said one, "In a way, it is possible that we will be 'crucified' by this decision."

Hobbs

Hobbs is a rapidly growing boom town, sprawled on the flat mesa land of southeastern New Mexico, its houses and streets running out into the surrounding oil fields. It is said locally that most of the residents have come from other oil areas of Texas and Oklahoma. The older residents trace their ancestors to Southern states. Although the 1950 census listed Hobbs' population as just under 14,000, current local estimates, based on school enrollment and utility connections, put it at nearer 20,000. Until recent years the town had a large transient population connected with the activities in the surrounding oil fields; since about 1947, however, there has been a rapid growth of new residential areas with more people establishing permanent homes. In 1950 nearly one-half of the people in Hobbs had lived there less than five years, and only 14 per cent had been there more than fifteen years. The population was younger than the national average.

The rapid growth of the town is indicated by the fact that until 1949 there were no paved streets other than the highways running through it, but by 1954 most of the streets were paved, with the exception of projects under way in the remainder of the present residential districts. South of the main thoroughfare many of the houses were small and poorly constructed, and there were in addition a large number of trailer homes. North of the main street was located the older residential neighborhood, and then, further from the center of town, the newer homes. The latter were substantially built and better kept than those south of the main street.

Of the total population, there were less than fifty Spanish-American families who lived in the southwestern quadrant of the city among Anglo-American neighbors. About 9 per cent of the total population was Negro, and the proportion had been relatively stable during the rapid growth of the area. Other than Albuquerque, a much larger city, Hobbs had more Negroes than any city in the state. Although there was no zoning ordinance, most Negroes lived in the southeastern quadrant of town. Their homes were small, many without inside plumbing, on still unpaved streets, and in the less well cared for sections. However, informants said that the majority of the houses were owner-occupied. Other residential areas in Hobbs had restrictive covenants in their deeds, so it was unlikely that any Negroes would be able to buy property outside this section, except in an area immediately adjacent to this section but north of the main street. A few Negro families had bought homes there, a residential pattern which was of current interest to the community in the school desegregation program.

Public facilities, with very few exceptions, were segregated in Hobbs. Hotels and motels did not accept Negro guests except during spring training season for the Big League teams, but at this time some hotels would accommodate a whole team. Some hotels and motels would also accommodate high school athletic teams with a bi-racial personnel. The restaurants frequently displayed the sign, "We reserve the right to refuse service to anyone," and informants in the community said that only a few restaurants would serve Negroes in the company of white patrons and then only in special rooms apart from the general dining room. The town had no local buses, but in buses passing through Hobbs, Negroes occupied the back seats.

There were no Negro clerks in the stores although during the harvest season some stores hired Spanish-American clerks for the serving of transient laborers. Informed persons reported that there were very few openings in employment for Negroes above the unskilled or semi-skilled level, with the exception of the school teachers and a very few plumbers and carpenters. There were two Negro policemen in the Negro section of town, and the city departments of water and sanitation hired a few Negro laborers. None of the oil companies, which furnished the major source of employment, hired Negroes; on the other hand, some persons in the Negro community said that the Negroes did not apply to the companies because they did not like the risks involved in the work.

Recreational facilities which were privately owned, such as a swimming pool, a bowling alley, a roller skating rink, were segregated. One movie had set aside a section for Negroes; the other two were completely segregated. Three drive-ins made no distinction. Recreational programs sponsored by the Chamber of Commerce, such as the Little League baseball teams, were integrated, with at least two Negro youth on each team. There were about two dozen such teams of boys under twelve in town. These were started about 1952 with very little parental protest over integration or heckling from patrons at the games. The Little League was credited here, as in the other towns in this area, with improving human relations through participation in sports.

The churches were segregated, and there was no organization which might have functioned in the field of intergroup relations. Perhaps because Hobbs had more than doubled its population in ten years, there were as yet very few civic organizations other than the men's service clubs, the Federated Women's Club, and a very few church groups interested in civic affairs. As one informant remarked, "It is still a young and growing place, and it's easy to interest individuals in getting things done, without running into cliques and groups already set in their ways."

The only interracial organization was a small chapter of the NAACP whose existence was unknown to all but a very few of the white residents although this group had been working toward desegregation of the one school for Negroes. It claimed about seventy members, but one leader said that less than two dozen were active. These active persons were known to the white community, but they were not recognized as local members of a national organization. One influential white informant considered them the "radical" part of the Negro community.

The first segregated school in Hobbs was constructed about 1933 as the result of a petition circulated among the small Negro community by one man who had a daughter qualified as a teacher. The school board at that time had told the Negroes that their children were welcome in any school in the town. By 1954 there was still one school for Negroes serving the community in all grades, with a Negro principal and a staff of sixteen teachers. The building was relatively new, well equipped, with a large gymnasium, and was the equal of any but the most modern in the system. It served approximately 400 students and was located in the center of the Negro neighborhood, about six blocks from another elementary school serving an adjoining white area.

In the fall of 1953 a small group of Negro parents took their children to one of the schools for whites and asked that they be registered there. The school administrators replied that under the law of the state they were maintaining a segregated system. The parents returned home, and nothing further was done during the school year.

A side issue, resulting in a slight amount of tension among the citizens interested in the schools, involved the firing of one white and one Negro teacher, both with tenure in the system. Each appealed the action, and the cases were still pending in the State Supreme Court in 1954. However, because there were representatives of each race involved, it was the opinion of both Negro and white informants that "race" was not the issue involved in either case.

In addition to the five-member Board of Education, Hobbs operates with a ten-member advisory committee, two members selected by each board member. By relying upon these two groups, the school administration felt that the decisions it made reflected as accurately as possible the sentiments of the community as a whole. The superintendent has been in office since 1947 and in the system since 1935. He was well known in the town.

Until the Supreme Court ruling was announced, the board had not considered the possibility of desegregation seriously although the need for strengthening and equalizing the facilities at Washington School had been the reason for that school being one of the first in the system to be modernized several years ago. Within a few days of the ruling, the board met to consider the implications of the decision and its effect on the New Mexico law. It called in the advisory committee and the board lawyer after the board's all-day session, and this second session also lasted a full day. The lawyer advised the board and the administration that in view of the court's ruling, the New Mexico law was now unconstitutional, and the board would be open to immediate suit if it did not desegregate the schools by the fall of 1954.

At the end of this meeting the board agreed unanimously to end segregation in the Hobbs system, effective in the fall of 1954. One member said later that though it was the feeling of the board that the Supreme Court's ruling must be followed, there were as many variations of personal feeling on the matter as there were board members. The school administrators were frank to admit that in the prolonged sessions all the possible means of avoiding the full implications of the decision were discussed, and they reported it was the unanimous decision of the board that such measures would only lead to further difficulty without accomplishing either segregation or desegregation.

When the decision to desegregate was reached, it was explicitly stated: the town would be districted as usual, taking into consideration walking distance from the schools and the capacity of the buildings; district lines should approximate natural boundaries as far as possible; and no transfers out of district would be allowed to avoid the integrated schools. The board had never in the past allowed transfers and did not see that the new situation would be improved by altering its firm policy. As in the past, some schools would be designated as bus schools for the rural children who came into town for their education, and the designation would continue to depend on the capacity of the school. However, in the future where there were some Negro children in the rural area, they would be taken to whichever bus school was designated for that area and not to Washington just because it was "the Negro school."

The new district lines, when drawn, indicated that there were fringe settlements of white families in the formerly Negro district and a few Negro families in the formerly white district. Both were areas of relatively low economic status, and it was not unusual for Negro and white children to play together in these neighborhoods. In fact, the gym at Washington School was a gathering place for all the youth of the district for square dancing, games, and other social activities. It was more adequate for a summer recreation program than was the school for whites near by.

The desegregation announcement was made through the newspaper and over the radio on May 23. It emphasized that the Negro teachers were being retained and that it was possible that they would be assigned to schools other than

Washington in the fall. The announcement also emphasized that the action of the board was being taken on the advice of the attorney and without such action the board would be subject to immediate suit for noncompliance with national laws.

There was no immediate public reaction to the announcement, but the board and the school administration estimated that 90 per cent of its time from then throughout the summer was spent on specific problems in relation to the process of desegregation. There were a number of extra board meetings, consultations with the advisory committee members individually and as a group, informal conferences with community leaders, and conferences among the school personnel.

At the time of the meeting of the board, May 20, the superintendent met with the Negro staff and told them that the entire staff, including those members not on tenure, would be retained. Two members had resigned, which left thirteen teachers and the principal. The following day they were given their contracts for the next year. In this way the administration avoided having wild rumors and uncertainty influence the opinions of the Negro staff. Before the decision of the board, some informed Negroes had said that the principal and some of the teachers had been quietly working against desegregation, thinking that their careers might be endangered should the schools be desegregated. The firing of the teacher in Las Cruces was well known. The superintendent announced that the junior and senior high school teachers at Washington School would be assigned to the two junior and the one senior high schools. The assignments placed two Negro teachers in each of the junior high schools and one in the senior high school.

The school administration had a tradition of friendly cooperation with the daily paper and the local radio station, and in addition to the initial release stating the change in policy with regard to segregation, there were news releases on June 6, 14 and 27 dealing with the point of view of the administration, the board, and the legal position of the system as the result of the Supreme Court decision. One release announced the renaming of most of the schools in the system; most of the changes were necessary to remove sectional designations now that there was more than one school in the district. However, the Booker T. Washington was to be called just the Washington School.

An extraneous factor in the publicity given the schools, however, had some local influence. In Hobbs there is also a weekly paper, which cannot, because of the immediacy of some news items, always carry "fresh" information. This has led to some rivalry between the daily and the weekly papers, and in the desegregation issue the rivalry was used to point up the problems involved. This is another example of how factors unrelated to the problem of desegregation can be used to draw otherwise disinterested individuals into a debate on the issue.

Indicative of the type of news releases from the school administration was a report of an interview with the superintendent which appeared in the daily paper on June 27. It read, in part:

[The] Superintendent . . . has told the Parent-Teacher's Association that he is "confident that the board of education would be glad to discuss the decision to end segregation in the Hobbs Schools with any group," but that he is equally confident that "the decision the board has made will have to stand, simply because no other decision is possible under the present law."

. . . In closing his talk, he said that, "the teaching of citizenship is one of the primary functions of the public schools, and that one of the most effective ways of teaching citizenship is to teach respect for law and order. One of the most effective ways to teach respect for law and order is to obey the law of the land. It is now the law of the land that separate schools for Negroes are unconstitutional."

Within a short time after the local policy change was announced, the superintendent met with the PTA of the elementary school most directly concerned in the change, explained the reason for it, and gave the opportunity for discussion of the board's decision. Several parents asked that: 1) the two districts most directly affected be thrown into one district, leaving choice of school up to the individual pupil; and 2) that the Negro teachers be shared equally by all the schools in the system. It was pointed out at the meeting that protests of this sort should stem from a citizens' group rather than from the PTA which was not organized to be in opposition to school policy. The rumblings at this meeting were the first indication of protest at the board's decision. It was the impression of the school officials who attended the meeting that the protests stemmed from a very few individuals who were not necessarily parents but landholders in the districts involved.

One condition of housing in these districts, peculiar to Hobbs and not encountered in any of the other communities studied, was the presence of a large number of trailer homes occupied by white families of oil field workers. There was some speculation that these families might be able to locate in other areas in or near the town, where the proportion of Negroes to be in the schools would be lower or where Negroes would be absent entirely. A lack of zoning made some such moves possible. There was also some indication that white families who owned homes in these districts were threatening to sell them in order to move to the north side of town or "move to Texas." However, a check with the real estate agents a month later showed that there were no more homes for sale in south Hobbs than was normal for that period of the year. Apparently the threats were words rather than actions.

In addition to Washington School, there were six elementary, one junior high, and one senior high school. Another junior high school in the southern quadrant of town was to be opened in the fall of 1954. It was estimated that when the fall term opened, there would be approximately 275 Negro pupils and perhaps twenty white pupils in Washington School which was being remodeled to be a completely elementary unit. In the elementary school closest to the more solidly Negro district, there would be approximately seventy Negro pupils, or less than 10 per cent of the total enrollment. One of the junior high schools expected about twenty, the newer one about seventy, Negro students. There were just over fifty Negro students to go to the high school. If there was to be the population mobility expected by some informants, it was possible that there would be fewer white students in Washington School and fewer Negroes in the junior and senior high schools. The latter prediction, made by some school officials, was based on the assumption that in spite of official school policy, the Negro youth might find the desegregated situation less appealing than the formerly segregated school had been.

The principal of Washington School was retained there as principal, and two white teachers were to be added to the staff. Each of the latter was told of his new assignment but neither was given a choice of assignment. In spite of some fears that a Negro would have a difficult time coaching in an integrated school, the coach from Washington School was assigned to a desegregated junior high school. No exceptions were made to the assignment of teachers on the basis of preparation for particular grade levels; each teacher from Washington was kept at the level for which he had been trained.

While to some of the citizens of Hobbs the decision of the board may have seemed hasty, there was a tradition already established within the schools of integrated activities, both with the students and with the faculty. Since 1947, faculty meetings, both formal and social, had been integrated, as had been professional activities and committees of teachers. There was also some tradition of integrated sports for the youth and of an integrated summer recreation program although both of these were relatively new to the town.

After the meeting with the PTA of the elementary school which would have approximately seventy Negro children in the fall, the administration was just beginning to think that its decision had been accepted. In the six weeks following the announcement there had been only sporadic protests from individual white parents. But on the morning of June 29 leaflets were distributed along with the home delivery of the *Ft. Worth Star-Telegram* announcing a meeting in a Protestant church in Hobbs for all those interested in the decision to desegregate the schools. This church was situated in a district unlikely to be affected by the changed policy, but it was in a low income neighborhood. However, it was said that some members of the church were residents of the southern quadrant of the city, and the pastor was known as a vigorous supporter of unpopular movements.

About 200 persons came to the meeting, some of them under the impression that it was sponsored by the Ministerial Alliance although informed persons said that most of the Protestant clergy had preached sermons containing favorable comments on the Court's decision. The meeting was called to order by the minister, who led the audience in a hymn and a prayer for the success of the undertaking. The treasurer of the committee announced that the meeting had been called because of the inconclusiveness of the PTA meeting with the school administration. He stated that the administration had not changed its policy as the group had asked and suggested that a further meeting with them be called. The minister then spoke at some length, quoting the Bible to show that "God drew the color line, God set segregation." He declared that since the voters of Hobbs did not like the Supreme Court decision, they could "just hand it right back to the Court; they did not have to obey a law which was contrary to the way of the Lord."

Issues other than desegregation as such came into the meeting. There were "amens" following any reference to the Bible. There were repeated statements that the daily paper did not publish the announcement of the meeting but that the weekly paper had offered full cooperation to the committee. Much time was spent impressing the group with the difference between the two papers. The final decision of the meeting, suggested by one of its organizers, was that a further meeting with the school board would be requested. At no time during this meeting was any proposal made as to how the board might meet the objections of the group without rescinding its decision to abolish segregation. Each speaker began with some version of, "Now I think it's perfectly right that the Negro children should be able to come to our schools if they want to, but. . . ."

The school board considered the possibility of meeting with a committee from the group but decided that it might be advisable to hold an open meeting to allow anyone who wished to speak out. This second meeting was held in the gymnasium of the high school on a Saturday night and drew approximately 600 persons. A small group of Negroes came to observe and stayed in spite of the many bitter remarks flung at the school officials by persons in the audience.

Between the two meetings the Segregation Committee had completely shifted its basis of argument. While they appeared to be willing to go along with the board's decision in some measure at the first meeting, at the second they demanded that the board rescind its decision and keep the Hobbs schools segregated. It was their argument that this could be done, no matter what the Supreme Court might say about it. Persons who attended the meeting said that as soon as a board member got up to speak, after the minister had talked for some time, a number of the audience left noisily. When the superintendent rose, a large share of the remaining audience did the same thing, and the meeting broke up in some disorder.

The school officials and the board held further meetings to discuss the reactions to the change in policy and to consider practical means of overcoming some of the objections to desegregation. They were aware of the fact that the organizers of the protest group were hoping that the board would put Negro teachers in each of the schools so that, as one protest leader expressed it, "Then the whole town will rise up and stop this thing; as it is, only the people in two districts are affected." The board felt that it was caught in a pincer movement; any retreat from its original decision would be unlikely to satisfy the protest group and at the same time might involve the board in litigation with some Negro families. It recognized a possibility of violence led by some of the more irresponsible persons in the community.

Interviews with leaders of the Segregation Committee, with Negro teachers and leaders of that sub-community, and with white parents whose children would be attending Washington School shed some additional light on the various points of view represented. One leader of the Segregation Committee stated that if they were able to get the board to keep the elementary schools segregated, then "we can teach our children the difference between black and white. Why, if they go to school with these darkies from the first grade, they just won't know that there is any difference in a few years."

The Negro community had been more shocked and alarmed over the first meeting, when they were unsure what the reaction of the school officials would be, than they were over the second one even though it was at the second meeting that threats of violence were made rather widely. They felt if the board held firm to its decision, the threats would not materialize.

One white mother, a Southerner recently come to Hobbs, stated that she saw no reason to object to having her little girl go to Washington School. She had been to the school and talked with some of the teachers and was impressed with their courtesy and their interest in the children who were playing in the gym and on the playing field. She thought that if the white parents in this district would teach their children not to abuse the Negro children and call them unpleasant names, everything would work out all right. However, she said that she was in a very small minority among her friends because she did not object to desegregation.

One factor was operating in Hobbs which had not been found in any of the other communities: a religious group opposed to desegregation on the grounds that it violated the teachings of the Old Testament. The leaders of this group did not accept the legal and practical grounds cited by the school board and the administration for the necessity of desegregation. Further, the revival meeting which took place during the period of the school discussions probably served to reinforce opposition. How much fervor was aroused by the revival meeting could only be inferred from the fact that three times as many persons came to the second protest meeting and that each meeting was led by the same minister. Whether these people would carry out their threats was the crucial question remaining at the end of the field study.

Clovis

Clovis is situated in the high plains of east central New Mexico, very close to the border of Texas. It was established as a railroad town early in the century, and it has prospered through ranching and irrigated agriculture in the surrounding area. In 1954 its population was estimated to be about

19,500, of whom approximately 400 were Negro and 600 Spanish-American.

Culturally Clovis is an Anglo-American town; by tradition the Spanish-Americans and the Negroes have lived in the southwestern quadrant of the city near the Santa Fe round-house and the stockyard. A few Spanish-American families in the higher socioeconomic levels have moved into other sections, but the Negro residential area has expanded much more slowly.

Employment for the minority groups was limited for a number of years to the roundhouse, the stockyard, or common labor. Some Spanish-Americans work in the feed mill but none in the flour mill. For Negroes, economic opportunities were more limited. However, there have always been a number of porters and waiters employed by the railroad, and this has tended to keep the economic level of the Negro community slightly higher than in other similar communities in the state. In recent years, the variety of jobs open to Spanish-Americans has increased, so that it is now not unusual to see them acting as secretaries in offices, clerks in stores, and in other skilled positions. Some have served as appointed or elected city and county officials. This has not been true for the Negroes. Other than the professional staff at the school for Negroes, there were no Negroes employed in professional activities in Clovis.

Most private facilities were closed to Negroes. However, in the last few years, some motels would accept teams with a bi-racial personnel; the main hotel would not. There was a Negro hotel in town. Restaurants did not serve Negroes, with the exception of a few persons who were members of men's service clubs because of their position in the schools. They were served when the clubs met for luncheons, but they did not at other times ask for service in these restaurants.

On the other hand, all movies except one would admit Negroes, and all city recreational facilities were open to everyone. An exception to this usual practice was a swimming pool in the park situated in the white residential area where Negro servicemen from the Clovis Air Base had been allowed to swim in the past. In the summer of 1954 another park was opened near the Negro and Spanish-American residential area, and the pool was open to all who wished to swim there. Its patrons were primarily youth of the area, including some of the Anglo-American children who lived nearer to it than to the other pool. This pool started a series of free swimming lessons, the first to be given in the city, and attendance was large. Soon after this program was undertaken, the other pool also gave free lessons. Both the director of this park and the coach at the swimming pool were Negroes employed on the teaching staff of Lincoln-Jackson School, the one which until the fall of 1954 had been exclusively for Negro children.

In addition to the active swimming program, there were Little League and Pony League baseball teams sponsored by service clubs in the town. These teams, through the summer of 1954, were on a segregated basis, but they played matches together. There was also an active sports program at Lincoln-Jackson in the high school department, and the basketball team here had played matches with Anglo-American teams although it had never played Clovis High School. Interest in sports seemed to have been stronger than feelings about racial separation on the part of the patrons of the different games.

Until the early 1920's, there had been no school for Negroes in Clovis. About that time one was started in the Baptist Church, with one teacher. Until six years ago, even after the Lincoln-Jackson School had been built, Negro children attended school only through the tenth grade. The first class of three to finish the twelfth grade graduated in 1950. At that time the school employed five teachers.

The principal of the school was considered by the white community to be the leader in the Negro group although many of his methods and interests outside the school were not approved by the Negro community. Each year for several years there was a petition to the school board for his removal signed by some members of the Negro group. When he retired in the spring of 1953, plans were made to expand the school and make it the equal of any in the system. Up to that time it had been functioning in some temporary barracks buildings and a gymnasium had been added the year before. The plans included a twenty-four room structure to house and educate all Negro youth through high school.

The impetus for the new building originated through a petition from the Negro community for the continuation of a Lincoln-Jackson School, with the facilities and equipment equal to that in the other schools. The Negro community felt that this was the most feasible way of achieving equal educational opportunities. However, the school board had considered the possibility of integrating the junior and senior high school youth on grounds of the expenditures necessary to provide facilities at this level. This proposal was not greeted with much enthusiasm in the Negro community because it meant that they would no longer have individual athletic teams, and they were very proud of holding state championships in several sports.

In the spring of 1954 the former superintendent of schools retired, and the new appointee was one who had been through the desegregation process in a neighboring town. When the Supreme Court decision was announced, the board had a prolonged meeting, and a decision to desegregate the Clovis schools in the fall of 1954 resulted. The public announcement was not made until early in July, and it dealt with the district lines and the schools by name, without mentioning that the new lines in effect desegregated the elementary as well as the secondary schools.

The plan to be followed in Clovis involved moving the Negro junior and senior high school students into the formerly segregated white schools, creating a new and larger elementary district which included the Spanish-American and Negro areas, and allowing children in that district to choose either the formerly all Spanish-American elementary school or the Lincoln-Jackson School. About twenty Anglo-American families, with approximately thirty school-age children, living in this section of town would also be sending their children to one of these schools. Formerly they had been allowed to choose another elementary school in a different neighborhood. The superintendent and the board felt that by allowing a choice of school in the initial transition, any protests which might come would be minimized. By the middle of the summer not one parent had protested to the school administration. Of the total school population in the spring of 1954 of about 4,200 students, 235 were Negroes in Lincoln-Jackson. It was estimated that in the fall of 1954 there would be about twenty-five Negro youth in the junior and senior high schools and approximately 210 in the elementary schools. Most of the elementary children would continue in Lincoln-Jackson, but a few were expected to go to La Casita, just as a few Spanish-Americans were expected at Lincoln-Jackson. Spanish-American attendance at the elementary levels was not as large as might be expected because of a parochial school in that district.

It was felt that in a year or so these two schools could each have a separate district as did the other elementary schools. By that time the new Lincoln-Jackson building would be completed; it was being built in three sections, one in the summer of 1954, one each summer following. By the fall of 1954 the school would have six new classrooms, in addition to the old ones, nine teachers, and a teaching principal. The Negro principal was very popular with the majority of the Negro community and with many of the Spanish-American children. Some of the Spanish-American youth had asked permission to attend this school before the decision of the board was announced. One school official commented, "The success of the desegregation program is in the hands of the Negro principal."

Except from the point of view of economic efficiency, the board had not been under much pressure from the community or from outside sources to desegregate the schools before the Supreme Court announcement. There had been some queries from the State Department of Education concerning the standards of Lincoln-Jackson in the past, even though it was an accredited high school. From the first few graduating classes, several students had gone on to college and done well. The desire of the Negro community to keep their own athletic team suited the majority sentiment in the community which appeared to favor segregation.

The school board did not take any action to integrate the teaching staff. All teachers at Lincoln-Jackson were qualified to teach at the elementary level with the exception of the coach who was considered a special case. All were given new contracts although only six of them were on tenure. One Negro school official expressed the opinion that if a Spanish-American teacher were hired to teach in that school, the Spanish-American children would have someone in whom to confide, and it would make it easier for them to adjust to a new situation. It was hoped that such a person could be found for the post. There were no teachers from this ethnic group in the Clovis schools. It was also hoped that there would be an Anglo-American attached to the Lincoln-Jackson School as secretarial or clerical help the first year, as another symbol of the sincerity of the board's actions. Apparently the possibility of placing a Negro teacher in La

Casita, the former all Spanish-American school which might now have Negro students, had not been considered.

The school administration and the teaching staff in the junior and senior high schools felt that there was a need to make the Negro youth feel welcome there in the fall of 1954. Some thought that the good Negro athletes would have the least difficulty in making the adjustment. However, informed members of the Negro community felt that the entering classes in the junior and senior high school would be smaller than they had been for several years before desegregation until the students saw that they would not be subject to discrimination. Several who might have been expected to go on in school had already joined the armed forces. No informant thought that this indicated a trend, however. It was said that under earlier administrations, Negro children had been taught that if they went to the white schools there would be race trouble, and in spite of the different attitudes on the part of recent school administrators, the feeling still persisted in the Negro community.

The methods used in Clovis are in contrast to those of Hobbs. Whereas Hobbs made a complete change in one move, including integrating the faculties, Clovis arranged for a more gradual process by leaving an open school district and keeping the Negro teachers in one school. It is possible that for Clovis this will not retard desegregation because two minority groups are represented in the district as well as a small number of white families. In Hobbs, had such a system been used, it would have been unlikely that any white children would have gone to Washington School although some Negro children would certainly have tried to register in the other elementary school.

The difference in publicity also deserves some comment. All releases by the Hobbs school administration stressed the fact that Hobbs was complying with the Supreme Court's decision. The widespread interest in the Court's decision and the rather sudden introduction of the words "segregation" and "desegregation" seem to have released some public emotion and created some confusion as to the exact meaning of each word. The one release in Clovis contained no mention of desegregation but announced the school districts and the plans for expansion in the various schools.

CHAPTER 11

Mission Accomplished
Tucson, Arizona *

The story of the integration of the Tucson public
schools centers around a man who worked toward this goal
for a number of years, steadily and with increasing support
from individuals and organizations in the city. The last step,
dramatic as it may have seemed to be under a permissive
law, was but the culmination of these years of preparation.

Almost 100,000 people live in the Tucson area, 45,454 of
them in the city proper in 1950. In the city itself about 6
per cent of the people are Negro, 20 per cent Spanish-American, and there are an appreciable number of Indians not
living on reservations. The majority of the population is
Anglo-American. Tucson has developed as a bi-lingual city
with the Spanish-Americans represented in all socioeconomic
levels. The more economically secure Spanish-American and
Anglo-American families mingle socially, and both have developed a paternalistic attitude toward the Indians. The
Negroes, most recent addition to the ethnic groups, are on
the bottom rung of the socioeconomic ladder, in competition
with the more recent immigrants in the Spanish-American
group.

* Based on the report of field research prepared by Edward P. and
Marianne Dozier, Northwestern University.

There is no history of any open conflict between the different ethnic groups in Tucson. The majority of the Anglo-American population is composed of recent arrivals who have not come predominantly from any one section of the country. Many of them who have come from areas where school segregation was never practiced did not favor segregation in Tucson. Other Anglo-Americans and the Spanish-American population in general appear to have been largely indifferent to the integration of Negro children.

Since early in this century, Tucson has been famous as a health resort; service to health-seekers is a major business. The lure of the warm, dry climate draws not only people who settle permanently, but also tourists for short or long sojourns. Since the last war, industry has also made its contribution to the economic life of the city in the form of aeronautical factories which have provided new types of employment. These factories have drawn an increasing number of Anglo-Americans to the area.

There are no solidly Negro residential areas. Negroes live primarily in the same neighborhoods as Spanish-Americans. Unlike the Spanish-Americans, however, they are limited to these neighborhoods no matter what their economic status may be. This status is usually low, because very few skilled or professional positions have been open to Negroes in the past. Only in the last few years, through the efforts of some labor unions and a few interracial organizations, have job opportunities increased.

The patterns of segregation and discrimination have never been completely consistent, and within the last few years they have been changing with increasing rapidity. This change has resulted, not from legal action, but from the persistent efforts of civic and interracial groups. Some motels will now accept Negro guests, as will some hotels, although the latter do so only during the Big League baseball training season. Most restaurants still refuse service to Negroes, but some do not object. Some drug stores serve Negroes at the soda fountain, others do not. Where theaters had balconies, Negroes were required to sit there; where there was no balcony, they could mingle with the other patrons. On this point, one theater manager said that the policy had been decided by the district manager in Phoenix and when the Phoenix policy changed, Tucson would do likewise.[1]

It is also important to point out that integration has been achieved in certain other community institutions. The YWCA has not excluded any ethnic or racial group in years, but the YMCA adopted a policy of integration only in 1950. Tucson's Medical Center and St. Mary's Hospital do not segregate their patients. The latter, moreover, now accepts Negroes for nurse's training. The Catholic parochial schools are operated on an integrated basis, and thus offer no retreat from public school desegregation.

Just a few months before the school integration program was announced, a committee from the local NAACP approached the city officials with a request that the public swimming pools be opened to Negro youth. The city council agreed to the request, but it made no public announcement of the change in policy. Actually, this was not so "revolutionary" a change, for the extra-curricular sports program of the schools had been on an integrated basis for several years, and the pools had been used by interracial groups in connection with school events. When desegregation was decided upon, members of the Negro community passed the information to their associates, and the day the pools opened, Negro youth were enjoying the facilities with no disturbances noted. No protests were recorded.

The Tucson public school system is much more simply organized than that of Phoenix. Here there are two school districts with coterminous boundaries, District 1 and High

1. Cornell University Studies of Intergroup Relations, Social Science Research Center.

School District 1. Each has a separate tax levy, but the work of the two districts is closely correlated and one board governs both. The school board consists of three members, one elected each year. Should a vacancy occur, the county superintendent of schools appoints a new member to fill the unexpired term. The superintendent of schools is appointed by the board. The schools are organized on a 6-3-3 plan. There are twenty-nine elementary schools, six junior high schools, and one high school.

Before integration, one of the schools served all Negro children up to the high school level. It had an enrollment of about 450 students and a staff of 21 teachers. The facilities of this elementary school, Dunbar, were considered by those who knew it to be equal in all respects to the white schools, and its teachers were as well qualified as any in the system.

Negroes were first segregated in the schools in 1914, and the Dunbar school was established in 1917. New rooms and facilities were added through the years, and a completely new building opened in 1950 with facilities equal to or superior to the other schools.

The high school had never been segregated completely although in the past there had been home rooms for Negroes only. This practice was discontinued a number of years ago.

The present superintendent of schools has held this position for more than ten years, and he had been associated with other schools in the area for many years. He is described as a man respected by his board, his staff, and the community in general. Shortly after he took office, he integrated such after-school activities as the sports program mentioned earlier in connection with the opening of swimming pools to interracial groups. He initiated interracial musical programs, such as band, orchestra, and choir. The effects of these changes seemed to reduce possible ethnic tensions and to make the school more representative of the community at large.

About five years before the permissive state legislation was passed, the superintendent had begun talking with his board, his administrative staff, and parent-teacher organizations about the wisdom of integrating the schools completely as soon as it was legally possible. He could see no reason for setting one racial or ethnic group apart from others already functioning harmoniously in school and extra-curricular activities.

In the spring of 1950 a number of initiative measures were presented to the voters of the state, among them a bill to make integration compulsory. The other measures had powerful opposition, and a "Vote No" psychology was created in the electorate. The school measure was defeated, many thought, because it had been presented along with the other proposals. Before the vote was recorded, the superintendent of the Tucson schools, speaking as an individual rather than in his official capacity, publicly espoused the bill. At that time it was said that he did not have the unanimous support of the school board on this issue. It is interesting to note that it was at this point, rather than later when integration became a fact, that protests were voiced. It is significant, too, that the protests were unorganized and came by way of anonymous letters and telephone calls. Opponents of integration here apparently were not willing to stand up and be counted publicly. It will be recalled that in several of the communities studied, opposition was vocal when initial proposals were made but not later when the change went into effect.

The organizations which had sponsored the bill praised the superintendent on his stand. These included the Tucson Council for Civic Unity, the Urban League Service Council, the local chapter of the NAACP, the Tucson Council of Churches, B'nai B'rith, and the Catholic Church. Locally and on the state level, the teachers' association, the Tucson Education Association, and the Arizona Education Association had been on record for several years as favoring desegregation. The AEA annually had presented a resolution at its meetings recommending desegregation of all Arizona schools.

Another persuasive and powerful agent for desegregation was the local press. Tucson's newspapers published editorials and gave favorable coverage to school integration news. Local press efforts preceded and accompanied Tucson's final step in the process of integration.

When, in the spring of 1951, it seemed likely that the permissive bill would pass the legislature, the superintendent met with the school board and presented plans for integration the following fall. Some members of the board were hesitant about an all-at-once approach, fearing community reaction. The superintendent maintained that it was morally right and economically sound to make the change in one move. He convinced the board, as one member reported later, because he had his plans well formulated and because the board had confidence in him and in his judgment of what was best for the schools.

Without the leadership and planning of the superintendent, the integration program could have stopped at this point. It might have been necessary, as it was in Douglas, to wait a year or more until the board could reach agreement or to pursue a policy of compromise such as that seen in some of the other communities.

Immediately after the bill passed, the superintendent met with the principals of the various schools, discussed plans, and asked for further suggestions. He and his staff were accustomed to discussing problems and reaching important decisions together. The staff supported him in his policies and in his administrative decisions. The following are excerpts from a talk given by him and appear to be typical of the quality of his communications soliciting cooperation for the integration of Tucson's schools:

We are confident that all of you will work together to make integration a reality rather than something superficial, and that all of you will continue to help us make the Tucson schools among the best in the nation. Teachers as well as boys and girls will need to adjust to their new schools and new environments.

We shall at all times consider all teachers as fellow citizens and fellow Americans, and all boys and girls as American boys and girls rather than as American Indians, Anglo-Americans, Negro-Americans, Spanish-Americans or Chinese-Americans.

We realize that most people have prejudices of one kind or another. We also realize that any change, no matter how good that change may be, will necessitate a revision of present practices. These problems will be a challenge to all of us, but I have every reason to believe that the challenge will be met in a fair, reasonable, and sensible manner.

After consultation with the principals, the superintendent let the Negro teachers know that he was going to ask for volunteers among his white teachers to accept assignments in the schools which would have the largest enrollment of Negro pupils. He emphasized that since teachers came from all sections of the country, it was possible that some might not wish to teach bi-racial classes, and he wanted to provide the most sympathetic teachers for the integrated schools. There were many more volunteers than were needed. Only one teacher asked to be placed in a school in which there would be no Negro pupils.

New school zones were worked out on the basis of capacity of buildings and nearness of pupils to them, with the result that most elementary schools would have some Negro children. The former school for Negroes was to be renamed for an educational pioneer in Arizona. It was agreed that in the future, when segregation would no longer be an issue, a new school would be named for a Negro leader.

The Spring School, formerly for Negroes only, was the

only one in which the proportion of Negro students exceeded 50 per cent. The proportion in the other schools ranged from less than 1 per cent to about 25 per cent. A few schools had no Negro students the first year because none lived near the school.

About six years before desegregation, the schools had initiated an orientation program for all children entering the elementary, junior high, or senior high school for the first time. The orientation program is a welcoming gesture to new students. It takes place in late spring and familiarizes the student with the school he is to attend in the fall. The program consists of class visits, introductions to teachers, and addresses by the principal and other members of the staff. In the elementary grades, parents are also invited to attend.

In 1951, Negro children and parents participated in the orientation program of their new school district for the first time. Weeks before orientation day, teachers had talked to their students about the benefits to be gained in the arts and humanities through association with varied ethnic groups. The importance of friendly and equal treatment of all persons was emphasized. Art teachers encouraged students in preparing posters welcoming "Our New Friends." The number of Negro parents and children who appeared for the program was not large, but those who came were impressed with the friendly atmosphere of all the schools.

In the spring and summer before the program was put into effect, the school administration was asked to provide speakers for civic groups. The superintendent accepted all invitations and gave most of the talks himself. When he was unable to attend, one of his staff made the speech. The press and radio reported favorably on these meetings.

The program went into operation in the fall of 1951, less than six months after the bill permitting it was signed. The Negro principal of the former Negro school was retained there as principal, but with an integrated staff and student body. Negro teachers were distributed throughout the system although no Negro teacher was placed in a school in which there were no Negro pupils. It was the feeling of the administration that this step would be better received at a later date. No transfers were permitted to students who might be seeking to avoid an integrated class. However, there were very few such requests.

Because the program in Tucson is regarded as definitely successful, it might be well to note some factors which, potentially, might have impaired its effectiveness. There was no organized resistance, but there were many individuals who did not favor integration. The superintendent was aware of that fact, but he acted to integrate at once.

A factor which might have discouraged a less determined man was the indifferent attitude of some of the Negro teachers. In interviews with them it was brought out that they were satisfied with the *status quo* before integration. They had been afraid that trouble might develop between whites and Negroes. Some felt that the Negro children were not prepared for an integrated school, either through scholastic achievement or emotional attitudes. The teachers were not openly opposed to the program, nor did they feel personally insecure over their future in the system. It was the lack of active support for integration that surprised local observers.

During the two years the program had been in operation, some teachers had expressed concern about the progress of the Negro students. These students, on the whole, had not performed as well as had been expected in class work. Teachers pointed out that their socioeconomic environment had not been as favorable as for other groups, and they believed this factor had influenced their scholastic achievement. It was reported that although teachers did not favor these students in the matter of grades, many gave the Negro children extra help and encouragement where possible.

A study of the integration process was made by a University of Arizona class in a course dealing with minority peoples about three months after the first integrated term started.[2] The study revealed no open friction between children of the three major ethnic groups. The teacher-student relationship was normal and the teachers interviewed expressed favorable attitudes toward the new situation.

The study also revealed that some parents were resentful of the program. A considerable number of them expressed objections to their children going to school with Negro children. It was chiefly from the Spanish-American parents that this objection came, and it may be that these attitudes indicate fears of competition as well as attempts of Spanish-Americans to identify with the established Anglo-American groups in the community.

In addition to the actions of the superintendent, other factors tended to be favorable to desegregation. Tucson is a city with a large Spanish-American population and a sizeable Indian and Oriental minority in the city and surrounding areas. These ethnic groups have always been represented in the schools. In some schools, the Spanish-Americans have been in the majority. Therefore the addition of yet another ethnic group into the elementary schools was not completely novel.

Tucson has never had serious conflict among the various groups. The Anglo-Americans, because they come from all parts of the United States, were not united on the issue. Interracial organizations were active in support of integration, and they represented all the ethnic and socioeconomic groups in the community. Support from the educational organizations apparently was effective in promoting a receptive climate of opinion among the citizens.

2. Phillip Angier, *et. al.*, "Committee Report on the Study of Desegregation," 1951. (Term paper for Anthropology 120; study directed by Dr. E. H. Spicer).

PART IV

Implications for the Future

CHAPTER 12

In Summary: Review and Prelude

IN REVIEWING THE EXPERIENCES OF THE TWENTY-FOUR COM-
munities reported on here, the following questions arise:
What clues do they offer to other communities that soon
may need to prepare plans concerning desegregation? Do
they give any indication of the types of problems involved
or the most acceptable solutions found to them?

A most striking immediate impression of an enormous
range of different solutions and experiences is created by the
examination of these communities from New Jersey to Arizona. Variety seems to be the keynote; local responsibility
and control in the public schools are again vividly illustrated.
The complexity of forces at work in each community is impressive, as is the delicate balance of factors making for
stability and for change.

Yet there seem to be underlying similarities and uniformities in the experiences of community after community in the
processes of desegregation and of resistance to it. Each situation is unique in some ways—but never in all ways. For this
reason, the lessons of experience in any one community
never can be applied in detail to another community; but
at the same time, there are always some common principles

that apply to many situations, if the local decision makers can look deeply enough to discern them.[1]

Response to Legal Decision

Initial reactions within the United States to the decision of the Supreme Court were generally rather matter-of-fact. Those who approved were restrained in their praise of the decision, recognizing that many years might elapse before desegregation became integration; many of those who opposed desegregation accepted the decision as a fact that had to be recognized, while warning that in many communities implementation would be a long process.

A week after the decision was announced the *New York Times* was able to report that the keynote speaker at the North Carolina State Democratic Convention was applauded when he said, "As good citizens we have no other course except to obey the law as laid down by the Court."[2]

After the initial reaction, there were various rumblings. It appeared entirely possible that Southern reaction at the state level might resist the implementation of the ruling. As in the individual communities studied in the preceding chapters of this book, both opposition and some measure of cooperation could be expected in the time to come.

How the net balance of such varying reactions will come out in the long run is by no means clear. It does seem certain that further desegregation will occur, and that many of the experiences reviewed in this book will be repeated in other communities, both in the South and elsewhere.

The process may seem slow or fast, depending on whether

1. For a compilation of propositions on intergroup behavior, see Robin M. Williams, Jr., *The Reduction of Intergroup Tensions*, Social Science Research Council, Bulletin 57, New York, 1947.
2. *The New York Times*, Sunday, May 23, 1954, p. 1.

it is resisted or welcomed. Divided reactions are to be expected among both whites and Negroes. Resistance or welcome does not, contrary to popular belief, precisely follow
the color line. Some Negro parents as well as teachers have
been inclined, in the past, to feel that unless the rest of the
community's public facilities were also non-segregated, the
child's exposure to desegregated education could create personal problems for him in the larger segregated environment
and at the same time expose him to damaging experiences in
the school. Not every parent wanted his child to be a
pioneer.

Many white parents and teachers who react from long
established custom are expected to exhibit reluctance, even
though an increasingly large number of white people have
come to feel that some change is due in public education
for Negroes.

*The community cases show, however, that desegregation
is an uneven, shifting process, not a sudden massive change.*
It has been pointed out repeatedly that, even though desegregation has been ordered by the Supreme Court, it probably will be a number of years before the segregated school
will be ancient history in many communities. For years to
come, communities here and there across the United States
will be dealing with complexities of segregation and desegregation resulting from contingent factors over which the
school administration has little or no control. And when desegregation has been accomplished, the development of truly
integrated school activities is a continuing process.

Again, it must be emphasized that each community has
its own special blend of factors that are at work to produce
integration or resistance to it. In some aspects, every community going through the process in the future will meet
the detailed problems in its own individual way. But the
central interest here is to find regularities that may be appli-

cable to many communities. What, then, are the uniformities? What are the conclusions to be drawn from them?

For the Community as a Whole

Local autonomy of public schools, an impressive fact of American history, is amply documented in the communities studied here. As Owen J. Roberts said:

The final burden and responsibility for our schools rests, however, upon the local citizens who operate and support them. These people need and deserve all the help they can get, and one of their greatest needs is for objective facts which will guide them toward wise decisions in the face of difficult problems. It was primarily with the needs of these practical "decision makers" in the field of education in view that the directors and officers of the Fund for the Advancement of Education decided to support the present study.[3]

However, local systems have been linked more and more together in larger systems. These consolidated systems have resulted, in many instances, in more uniform standards. Increasingly, common policies are followed across the country, even though the final decisions are made locally.

Recent moves toward integration have resulted from forces both external and internal to the communities involved. External considerations, on a national and international level, are reflected in diffused individual attitudes; they are not focused on any one local problem unless there is a catalyst within the community. This catalyst may be as uncomplicated as the formation of a Little League baseball team or as complex as the location of a new school. There are always situations and processes internal to the community that powerfully affect its responses—the economic base for the community as a whole and for its schools, the functioning of its leadership, and the communication between groups.

3. Harry Ashmore, op. cit., p. vi.

For the Schools

Where the white community is not strongly opposed or where attitudes are unstructured, confused, and in flux, decisive importance attaches to the policies and actions of school boards and school officials. In such instances these gatekeepers can tip the balance one way or the other in the degree of ease with which the transition is made. Outstanding examples from the studies are Tucson, where the superintendent had his plans ready to put into action at the earliest possible moment; Douglas, Arizona, where the superintendent was willing to wait a year until he had the unanimous support of his board before announcing a change; Elkhart, where a school board was convinced by a reasoned appeal; and Cairo, where resistance was tinged with bitterness and the transition fraught with tension.

A tendency frequently observed in communities where desegregation initially aroused opposition was a lack of communication between white and Negro leaders and a tendency on the part of the whites to attribute the local call for desegregation to "outsiders." Sometimes responsibility was imputed to national organizations having a local branch or chapter. Sometimes the reaction took the form of "our own Negro people are satisfied with things as they are—it is only those outsiders who want change." Where definite information was available, however, it usually showed that among the local Negro people there were proponents of integration and that the white members of the community did not always have the full knowledge of the hopes and feelings of their Negro co-residents.

Both the removal of legal and customary arrangements for separation (desegregation) and the establishment of mutually acceptable shared participation (integration) are best thought of as processes rather than suddenly achieved end-conditions. One does not "push a button" and effect an over-night change. Desegregation is only a preliminary step; integration is the continuous process of achieving and maintaining cooperative association in which people share *compatible* values and goals.

The unevenness with which desegregation and integration have proceeded in the communities studied is shown by the fact that what happens in the school does not necessarily lead to important immediate changes outside the school. In most of the towns observed, educational integration has not yet had time to show whether it will affect other aspects of community life. Undoubtedly the changes in the schools are related to the general trend which has increased the participation of Negroes on school boards and in integrated PTA's, as well as in some other community activities.

Transition from segregation to non-segregation—and to some measure of true integration—took place in most of the twenty-four communities with a smoothness and lack of open friction which typically surprised officials and teachers. In this the public schools shared the same reactions found in Southern universities. In nearly all instances, the amount of difficulty and tension actually experienced was less than had been anticipated and predicted. Only in one town— Cairo, Illinois—was there any violence, and even in this instance no blood was shed. There was some evidence also that the violence in this case resulted partly from a configuration of *other* community tensions which were focused temporarily on an unpopular move.

The "medicine of nature" which operates in such instances should not be underestimated. Few communities of the kinds described here can sustain, over protracted periods of time, intense bitterness and tension involving only one of the functions of the community. The natural processes of spontaneous control and social adjustment absorbed the impact of change rather quickly. What was news one day, and news of a kind to stir heated comments, both official and informal, soon became another back-page item in the newspaper. Active resistance gave way to passive resistance, and that in turn became relative indifference or positive acceptance.

The implications of this point in respect to the entire nation are worth attention. Because the recent cases decided by the Supreme Court had been discussed publicly, in articles, forums, and in free discussions on a more informal level for two years before the decision was announced, individuals had time to adjust their thoughts and attitudes to the possibility of desegregation. That more time will elapse, and with it more discussion and opportunity for planning, before implementation of decrees governing the forms desegregation may take in the Southern states will mean that in some cases the impact of the idea of impending change will have been absorbed before desegregation actually occurs. It is also true, as some of the communities here studied attest, that this time span gives opportunity for opposition to crystalize and for community cleavages to develop. Instances of both outcomes are to be expected. Which will occur in particular communities depends upon factors already discussed at various points in preceding chapters. There is no substitute for careful local diagnosis.

Among the significant factors to consider in making an initial diagnosis of a particular community are:

1. Number and proportion of Negroes.

2. Presence of other "minority" racial or cultural groups.

3. Extent and nature of segregation and discrimination in public facilities and activities other than the schools.

4. Activity of organizations dealing with intergroup relations, local and non-local.

5. Organization and financing of the school system.

6. Amount and kind of communication between school board and administration and other citizens, and between Negroes and whites.

7. Employment status, tenure, and qualifications of white and Negro teachers.

8. Local attitudes toward the schools and their leadership.

9. Policies and practices of state agencies concerned with public education.

10. Role of local groups such as churches, service clubs, and civic organizations.

For example, as these studies repeatedly have shown, segregation in the school system is powerfully supported by the larger patterns of segregation of Negroes and whites, especially by residential segregation. Succinctly stated by Harry Ashmore, "Residential segregation creates a slum atmosphere, which reinforces the race prejudice of the community at large, which in turn is translated into the public attitudes which insist upon residential segregation." [4]

For most of the communities analyzed here, a much more specific point is also apparent. Residential segregation necessarily results in "fringe areas" in which some whites and Negroes live in close proximity. Typically also, portions of these areas contain intermingled residences of whites and Negroes, resulting either from the settlement of whites around an area of Negroes' dwellings or from the extension of Negro occupancy outward from a crowded area of concentration. If, then, districts for elementary schools are drawn on a purely geographic basis, the consequence usually is that either Negroes or whites will be in the great majority for any given district. Therefore, the families *directly* affected by desegregation in such situations will be the relatively small number living in "border" or "transitional" zones. Although there are, of course, exceptions to this pattern, it does seem to be a very common situation and one with important implications for the whole process of desegregation.

Another significant general finding is that public school

4. *Ibid.*, p. 77.

desegregation or integration is only loosely correlated with the attitudes or prejudices of the population. Successful public school desegregation has been carried out in places where supposedly the prevailing attitudes favored segregation and where other institutions continued to be segregated, such as Indianapolis; Mount Holly, New Jersey; and Gary, Indiana. Segregation has persisted for years in other instances where attitudes were *relatively* favorable for integration, such as Cincinnati, Camden, or Atlantic City. In some instances, as in Douglas, Arizona, school desegregation was successful in a completely segregated environment. Without a careful local diagnosis it is impossible to predict whether the school or some other local institution will move first toward integrated activity.

In those communities in which there was a tradition of activity in intergroup relations, and in which during the past decade such organizations as a mayor's friendly relations committee or human relations committee was active, the transition from segregation to desegregation seemed to have been made with relative ease. Such organizations were favored by a permissive community setting. Once active, they were able to lead in the discussion of the problem, furnish speakers for forum and other discussion groups, and in other ways help create the necessary favorable climate of opinion and leadership during the transition. Some communities made more direct use of such agencies than did others, depending on the tradition of cooperation between them and the schools. In some of the smaller communities where such interracial groups were inactive, the human relations aspects of desegregation were handled directly by the school administration.

A variety of procedures used in some of the communities results in retarding or minimizing desegregation even when the public policy seems to favor it. The most critical of these concerns districting. For example, "school of choice" under conditions of residential segregation, tends to retain segregation and to put the psychological "burden of proof" upon Negro parents and children. It also leaves the way open for the white children of higher socioeconomic level (those who can afford the extra expense involved in extra travel) to retreat to more remote schools as the near-by schools increase in Negro enrollment.

At the other pole a clear policy of geographic districting, with minimal allowance for "hardship" transfers, gives decisive force to the integration of schools. In some of the communities, an initially flexible policy was changed to a stricter one as it became too much of a burden to arrange transfers to pacify small dissident groups on the margins of school districts.

This last point has a wider application. In general a clear-cut policy, administered with understanding but also with resolution, seems to have been most effective in accomplishing desegregation with a minimum of difficulty. Long-drawn-out efforts and fluctuating policies appear to have maximized confusion and resistance. Even in those states which allowed either segregation or non-segregation, as in Indiana where the law permitted gradual change, interpretations of the legal position varied widely and application of the law apparently was subject to more criticism than where no alternatives were left open.

Some school administrations attempted to avoid all publicity; others cooperated fully with news agencies. The deciding factor in each case seemed to be the customary procedures within the school administration in regard to publicity in other aspects of school life. Publicity seemed to be a complex, rather than a simple variable. In some instances the school administrations shared their decision-making powers with a citizens' committee or with the general public through open meetings or forums. These seemed to have been successful where the administration and the board kept control of the situation, but where the citizens' committees were organized independently, without an invitation from the administration, there was indication of community resistance to desegregation. Once the board reached a decision, open meetings to explain the nature of the change in the school system usually resulted in its acceptance. News releases through press and radio were uniformly favorable to school administrations, except during periods of initial hesitation. Editorial comment on desegregation was uniformly favorable.

Statistics on the number and proportion of Negro children who were desegregated in each of the communities and on the extent to which they were really integrated into the school activities must, perforce, be educated guesses, since records of this kind vary from place to place or are not kept at all. From the evidence at hand it seems that the majority of Negro children in the states included in this study still live and go to school in segregated environments, but the last decade has seen this begin to change rather rapidly. Where desegregation has been in operation a number of years and where community attitudes have come to accept it as natural and normal, integrated extra-curricular participation has increased.

If desegregation does take place and there are white parents who object, they will be alert to any aspect of the assignment of white children to schools or classes with Negro pupils that can be interpreted as "favoritism." As Gary and Indianapolis show, partial desegregation that affects only one or a few schools in a community opens the door to charges that "we are being asked to do this, but the others aren't." This is one of the consequences of gradual desegregation that may not always be foreseen. A similar process can occur *within* a particular school, where some classes or rooms contain Negroes and others do not, unless an obviously impartial and objective procedure of selection was used. It was apparently to forestall charges of favoritism in such a situation that Salem, New Jersey, used a random method of assignment.

Many Negro pupils feel especially high motivation to prove their ability and good behavior in the integrated situation. In a number of the communities it was apparent that the Negro students were taking the initiative, with the help of interested Negro adults, in easing the transition. Most reports indicated that they tended to keep themselves apart unless sought out for the more informal activities connected with school or for social occasions. Some—probably fewer—Negroes reacted by initial sensitivity and over-compensating behavior. Aggressive behavior on the part of Negro youth was reported only from those schools in which the initial transfers were not handled in a sympathetic manner or where the extra-curricular activities continued to be segregated.

Pupil-to-pupil friction between whites and Negroes generally has been slight. A reiterated comment from nearly all communities was that if the parents did not interfere, the children got along all right. What evidence there is points to an impersonal friendliness in school and school-related activities, along with some withdrawal to like-groups after school. Again, only in the communities in which there was overt resistance to desegregation were there initial reports of friction, and these apparently resolved into the live-and-let-live attitudes described above.

In a sizeable but unknown proportion of instances Negro pupils have been hurt or embarrassed by deliberate remarks or unwitting "slips" on the part of white teachers. Unless the channels of communication are open in both directions (from the student to the administration and the reverse) these instances do not come to the attention of the school authorities. Sometimes an increase in "incidents" in a school can be traced to such lack of communication. Where the channels are blocked, the administration has no direct way of knowing if work in human relations is or is not needed in the schools among staff and students.

The use of Negro and white teachers with bi-racial classes in an integrated system tends to pose complex questions, and a great variety of patterns have been tried. Some communities like Las Cruces, dismissed the Negro teachers rather than use them in the integrated schools. Others have kept the Negro staff in the segregated schools, using only white teachers in the desegregated ones. Still others, like Cincinnati, have used both races in the elementary schools only. And finally, places like Tucson, Atlantic City, Elkhart, and a few others have placed the teaching staff according to ability and training without regard to race. In some of the smaller communities, where there were only a few Negro teachers in the first place, they have been rotated from school to school with special assignments to give all children an opportunity to participate in a bi-racial situation or for other reasons. This is true for some of the smaller communities in southern New Jersey and also in some of the Indiana communities.

The studies show that in the actual situation of faculty integration, where it has been tried, professional standards soon take precedence over previous racial attitudes. Teacher-to-teacher relations, over a period of time, come to be carried out in the normal professional way according to the usual customs among teachers. Interpersonal relationships develop according to shared interests and personal choice.

Where public school desegregation was made in communities in which residential segregation was prominent, immediate assignment of white and Negro teachers to schools or classes predominantly of the other race provided the initial step toward full integration by giving the students some experience in interracial communication and participation. The experience in southern New Jersey was that this was possible without delay when the public schools adopted such a program with tact and firmness. Such communities as Burlington, Camden, Atlantic City, Salem, and others have begun this process successfully.[5]

If there is no early discussion of the position or retention of the Negro staff under a proposed desegregation program, the Negro professional often fears for his job and promotion opportunities. In some instances these fears have been justified by later events, effectively limiting the expectation of professional security under the new system. Where these fears were well grounded, there often was resistance to the change among Negro teachers as strong as that put up by the whites. There is some inconclusive evidence that Negro teachers and principals fared better in the larger cities and in those with a higher proportion of Negro students. Where the proportion of Negro students was small as was the Negro staff, no new Negro teachers were hired as vacancies occurred.

At the teacher-student level, the children become not so many Negroes and whites as children who are to be taught. There is some evidence that Negro students, especially at the high school level, perform better in classes and are involved in fewer incidents either in class or on the school grounds when the faculties are at least partially integrated. These students understand more clearly than younger children the implications of a segregated faculty even when the student body is bi-racial.

Teacher-student relations show in the main that Negro teachers who are professionally well-qualified tend to be accepted by their white pupils, both in elementary and high schools, and that white teachers who can master whatever prejudices they have usually gain the acceptance of the Negro pupils. In many of the communities trying integrated

5. John Hope II, Some Case Studies of Public School Desegregation in New Jersey (unpublished manuscript), p. 156.

faculties, the best qualified teachers from both races were put in the bi-racial schools to ease the transition period. That this policy was successful is indicated by the comments of students and parents interviewed in the course of the studies.

There is an important difference between a change in actual behavior and the anticipation of a change. A direct challenge to customary ways typically arouses anxiety and resistance. The actual change usually removes vague apprehensions, substituting for them concrete problems in operation. The decisions made in this context become part of a public interest in maintaining a living community.

All human conduct is partly guided by "rules of the game" which help to define what conduct is appropriate and expected in particular situations. A clear definition of law and policy by legitimate social authorities may reinforce willingness to conform to the requirements of new situations. Persons coming into an unfamiliar situation, such as that experienced in initial desegregation, will be unusually sensitive to cues as to what is the appropriate and acceptable behavior. Hence the great importance of clarity and decisiveness in early policy and practice in the desegregation process cannot be overemphasized.

Important social changes generally do not occur without some resistance and friction. School desegregation is no exception. The change involves established interests, operating customs, cherished beliefs, and deep sentiments. It also poses a number of technical, economic, and administrative problems, even from a purely educational point of view. As the South begins what undoubtedly will be a gradual and uneven movement toward integration, there will be some incidents of personal conflict and name-calling—even instances of disturbances such as those in Cairo. There will be hurt feelings among children, Negro and white. There will be hectic days for school officials and parents. All these things have been seen in some of the communities reviewed in this book.

Nevertheless, the experience now at hand shows that where desegregation has been tried, the typical outcome has been its eventual acceptance. While the ease of transition varies greatly from community to community and some resist the move more than others, the direction of change is clearly toward the acceptance of educational integration as public policy.

Finally, it must be stressed again that desegregation and integration are not fixed or rigid conditions but moving and growing patterns. Even, or perhaps especially, tension and conflict can become opportunities for learning new skills, new concepts, and new values. No detailed prophecies can be made here as to the long-term future of integration in the schools. Unless our experience to date has been wholly misleading, however, a generation from now the people of the United States may be able with some pride to look back on this period as a time of successful transition, accomplished in a characteristically American way.

Appendices

Appendix I

12940. Penalty for denial of privileges at inns and other places by reason of color or race. —Whoever, being the proprietor or his employee, keeper or manager of an inn, restaurant, eating house, barber shop, public conveyance by air, land or water, theater, store, other place for the sale of merchandise, or other place of public accommodation or amusement, denies to a citizen, except for reason applicable alike to all citizens and regardless of color or race, the full enjoyment of the accommodations, advantages, facilities or privileges thereof or, being a person who aids or incites the denial thereof, shall be fined not less than fifty ($50.00) dollars nor more than five hundred ($500.00) dollars or imprisoned not less than thirty (30) days nor more than ninety (90) days, or both.[1]

1. Pauli Murray (ed.), *State Laws on Race and Color*, Woman's Division of Christian Service, 1951, pp. 352-353.

Appendix II

AN ACT establishing a public policy in public education and abolishing and prohibiting separate schools organized on the basis of race, color or creed, and prohibiting racial or creed segregation, separation or discrimination in public schools, colleges and universities in the state of Indiana and prohibiting discrimination in the transportation of public school pupils and students.

(H. 242. Approved March 8, 1949)

Be it enacted by the General Assembly of the State of Indiana:

Section 1. That it is hereby declared to be the public policy of the State of Indiana to provide, furnish, and make available equal, non-segregated, non-discriminatory educational opportunities and facilities for all regardless of race, creed, national origin, color or sex; to provide and furnish public schools and common schools equally open to all and prohibited and denied to none because of race, creed, color, or national origin; to reaffirm the principles of our Bill of Rights, Civil Rights and our Constitution and to provide for the State of Indiana and its citizens a uniform democratic system

of common and public school education; and to abolish, eliminate and prohibit segregated and separate schools or school
districts on the basis of race, creed or color; and to eliminate
and prohibit segregation, separation and discrimination on
the basis of race, color or creed in the public kindergartens,
common schools, public schools, colleges and universities of
the state.

Section 2. The School Commissioners, superintendents,
trustee or trustees of any township, city or school city or
county or state or any other public school, college or university official or officials, shall not build or erect, establish,
maintain, continue or permit any segregated or separate
public kindergartens, public schools or districts or public
school departments or divisions on the basis of the race,
color, creed or national origin of the attending pupil or
pupils.

Section 3. Where separate public kindergartens, public
schools, common schools or school districts, departments or
divisions are established, separated or segregated on the
basis of race, color or creed of the pupil or pupils, that said
officials of said public kindergartens and public schools, districts, departments or divisions shall at the beginning of
the September, 1949 school year and thereafter, discontinue
enrollment on the basis of race, creed or color of students
entering for the first time the public kindergartens, the first
grades of elementary schools and first year departments of
senior high or junior high schools; but said first year pupils
shall be permitted to enter and shall be enrolled in the
kindergarten within their district, the elementary school
within their district, and shall be free to enroll and attend
any public junior high school or senior high school of their
choice within the limitations applicable alike to all students
regardless of race, creed or color; provided that in schools
or districts where equipment and facilities are not available

for the enrollment and integration of such first year students in September, 1949, the period for the enrollment in the schools of their districts may be delayed or extended until the September, 1950 school year in the case of kindergarten and grade schools, the September, 1951 school year in the case of junior high schools, and the September, 1954 school year in the case of high schools, and that on and after the beginning of each of such school years, respectively, such students shall be enrolled in the schools of their District, and shall have and receive credit for such school work as has been completed and shall be certified by the transferring school.

Section 4. All students and pupils attending and enrolled in separate public or common schools, kindergartens, junior high schools, high school, colleges and universities after the respective dates set out in Section 3 of this act applicable to kindergarten, grade schools, junior high schools and senior high schools shall henceforth be admitted and enrolled in the public or common school in their districts in which they reside without regard to race, creed or color, class or national origin; and no student or pupil shall be prohibited, segregated or denied attendance or enrollment to any public school, common school, junior high school or high school in his district, or college or university in the state because of his race, creed, color or national origin, but shall be free to attend any public school, department or division thereof or college or university regardless of race, creed, color or national origin, and within the limitations and laws applicable alike to non-citizens and non-resident students.

Section 5. That no public school, college or university, supported in whole or in part by public funds of the State of Indiana or any township, town, county or city school or city thereof, shall segregate, separate or discriminate against in any way, any student or students therein on the basis of race, creed or color, nor shall admission to any such public school be approved or denied on the basis of race, creed or color.

Section 6. No public school, college or university supported in whole or in part by public funds of the State of Indiana or any township, town, county or city or school city or any other school official or officials thereof, shall discriminate in any way in hiring, upgrading, tenure or placements of any teacher on the basis of race, creed or color.

Section 7. The Board of School Commissioners, trustees or officials of any public school district or unit may provide suitable transportation, by proper conveyance to transport any and all children, regardless of race, creed or color or national origin from their home to their district school and back to their home or from school to school, under such regulations or rules as said officials shall set up and establish applicable alike to all regardless of race, creed, color or national origin of said student or students; Provided, That transportation shall in no instance be provided where the distance to be traveled by a student is less than one (1) mile.

Section 8. The provisions of the Act shall be deemed supplemental to any and all existing common law or statutory law or Civil Rights on the subject of public schools, common schools, colleges or universities, and rights and remedies thereof of the State of Indiana and the people thereof.

Section 9. If any section, paragraph, sentence or clause of this Act shall for any reason be held invalid or unconstitutional by any court of competent jurisdiction, the same shall not affect the validity of this Act as a whole, or any part thereof, other than that portion so held to be invalid or unconstitutional.

Section 10. All laws or parts of laws in conflict with this Act are to the extent of such conflict hereby repealed and the Acts of 1869 (Spec. Sess.), ch. 16, par. 3, p. 41; 1877, ch. 81, par. 1, p. 124; 1935, § 296, par. 1, p. 1457, are hereby specifically repealed.

Section 11. That whereby an emergency exists, all provisions of this Act shall be in force and effect September 1, 1949.

Appendix III

Ch. 122, Sec. 15-15. Exclusion of children on account of color.—sec. 15-15. Any school officer or other person who excludes or aids in excluding from the public schools on account of color, any child who is entitled to the benefits of such school shall be fined not less than five ($5.00) nor more than one hundred ($100.00) dollars.[1]

Ch. 122, Sec. 15-16. Preventing colored children from attending school.—sec. 15-16. Whoever by threat, menace or intimidation prevents any colored child entitled to attend a public school in this State from attending such school shall be fined not exceeding $25.00.[2]

1. Hurd's Rev. Stats. 1874, Ch. 122, p. 983, secs. 100, 101; L. 1889, p. 340, sec. 14; L. 1909, p. 342, sec. 261; Jones Ill. Stats. Ann., 123.1004.
2. Hurd's Rev. Stats., 1874, Ch. 122, p. 983, sec. 102; L. 1909, p. 342, sec. 262; Jones Ill. Stats. Ann. 123.1005.

Appendix IV

Ch. 122, sec. 6-37. (Powers of Board of School Directors) Assignment of pupils to schools—... Race Discrimination.— ... No pupil shall be excluded from or segregated in any such school on account of his color, race, or nationality.[1]

Ch. 122, sec. 7-14. (Powers of Board of Education) Appointment of pupils to schools—Race Discrimination.—sec. 7-14 ... No pupil shall be excluded from or segregated in any such school on account of his color, race, or nationality.[2]

1. L. 1909, p. 342, sec. 115, as amended by act approved July 17, 1945; L. 1945, p. 1593; Jones Ill. Stats. Ann. 123.811.
2. L. 1871-72, p. 737, sec. 80, as amended by act approved July 17, 1945; L. 1945, p. 1593; Jones Ill. Stats. Ann., 123.844.

Appendix V

18: 14-2. (1948 Cum. Supp.) —Exclusion on account of religion, nationality or color a misdemeanor. —No child between the ages of four and twenty years shall be excluded from any public school on account of his race, creed, color, national origin, or ancestry. A member of any board of education who shall vote to exclude from any public school any child, on account of his race, creed, color, national origin or ancestry shall be guilty of a misdemeanor, and punished by a fine of not less than fifty ($50.00) dollars nor more than two hundred fifty ($250.00) dollars, or by imprisonment in the county jail, workhouse, or penitentiary of the county in which the offense has been committed for not less than thirty days (30) nor more than six (6) months, or by both such fine and imprisonment in the discretion of the court.

18: 13-19. (1948 Cum. Supp.) —Tenure provisions not to prevent reduction in force; seniority; preferred list. —Nothing contained in Sections 18: 13-16 to 18: 13-18 of this Title shall be held to limit the right of any school board to reduce the number of supervising principals, principals or teachers employed in the school district when the reduction is due to a natural diminution of the number of pupils in the district. Dismissals resulting from such reduction shall not be by reason of residence, age, sex, marriage, race, religion, or political affiliation. . . .[1]

1. L. 1909, c. 243, sec. 3, p. 399 (C. S. p. 4764, sec. 106c), as amended by L. 1935, c. 126, p. 331, sec. 1, supp. to L. 1903 (2d Sp. Sess.), c. 1, p. 5, as amended L. 1942, c. 269, p. 713, sec. 1.

Appendix VI

55-1201. . . . Separate schools for colored pupils —Restriction. —Pupils who are residents of a district shall be permitted to attend school in the same regardless of the time when they acquired such residence, whether before or after the enumeration. Provided, that where, in the opinion of the county school or municipal school board and on approval of said opinion by the state board of education, it is for the best advantage of the school that separate rooms be provided for the teaching of pupils of African descent, and the said rooms are so provided, such pupils may not be admitted to the school rooms occupied and used by pupils of Caucasian or other descent. Provided, further that such rooms set aside for the teaching of such pupils of African descent shall be as good and well kept as those used by pupils of Caucasian or other descent, and teaching therein shall be as efficient. Provided, further, that pupils of Caucasian or other descent may not be admitted to the school rooms so provided for those of African descent.[1]

1. Laws 1923, ch. 148, sec. 1201, p. 290; 1925, ch. 73, sec. 21, p. 99, C. S. 1929, sec. 120-1201.

Bibliography

Anzier, Phillip, *et al.* Committee Report on the Study of Desegregation. Unpublished paper, Anthropology 120, University of Arizona, 1951.

Ashmore, Harry, *The Negro and the Schools.* Chapel Hill, University of North Carolina Press, 1954.

Boone, Richard G., *A History of Education in Indiana.* New York, D. Appleton and Co., 1892.

Lansden, John M., *A History of the City of Cairo, Illinois.* Chicago, R. R. Donnelley and Son, 1910.

Leflar, Robert A., and Wylie H. Davis, "Segregation in the Public Schools," *Harvard Law Review*, Vol. 67, No. 3, January, 1954.

Murray, Pauli (ed.), *State Laws on Race and Color,* Woman's Division of Christian Service, 1951.

Stouffer, S. A., *et al., The American Soldier*, Vol. I. Princeton, Princeton University Press, 1949.

Tipton, James H., *Community in Crisis, the Elimination of Segregation from a Public School System.* New York,

Bureau of Publications, Teachers College, Columbia University, 1953.

Wright, Marion Thompson, *The Education of Negroes in New Jersey*. New York, Bureau of Publication, Teachers College, Columbia University, 1941.

Williams, Robin M., Jr., *The Reduction of Intergroup Tensions*. New York, Social Science Research Council, Bulletin 57, 1947.

Index

www.ingramcontent.com/pod-product-compliance
Lightning Source LLC
Chambersburg PA
CBHW020339270326
41926CB00007B/250